Tuxedos and Pickup Trucks

FOREVER RIDING ON THE SOUTH WIND

Bill Thompson

Copyright © 2019 by Bill Thompson

Library of Congress Control Number: 2019949173

ISBN: 978-1-7333252-6-4 (soft cover)

Thompson. Bill
Tuxedos and Pickup Trucks

Edited by: Amy Ashby
Cover photo is courtesy of Doug Sasser.
The pickup truck featured on the cover is a
1955 Chevy owned by Eddie Pierce.

PipeVine
P R E S S

Published by PipeVine Press
Charlotte, NC
www.warrenpublishing.net
Printed in the United States

*Dedicated to the memory of Bill Thompson Sr. and
Mildred Thompson who made it all possible.*

Acknowledgments

Writing a memoir, particularly one that is based on recollections of relationships with other people, naturally requires a lot of assistance. I am particularly appreciative of the time so many family members and friends took to help me remember and to reminisce about places and events. The editors of Our State and Salt magazines were gracious enough to let me glean from old stories I had written for those publications. Sometimes the original story I had written for the magazine was the basis for a subsequent long and personal relationship with the subject.

I am most grateful to Mindy Kuhn and Amy Ashby at PipeVine Press for their encouragement and belief in this effort. I am particularly grateful to Amy as my editor. I was very fortunate to have a native of New Jersey remind me that many of my readers would not know that tobacco gum, that sticky substance on the tobacco plant, was very unlike any gum they had ever chewed; that so many of the esoteric terms I used would confuse anybody not familiar with the rural South. She made my memories readable, helped my readers connect with a time and place and each person I was writing about, and helped me focus on the stories that emerged.

My mother, Mildred Thompson, died while I was writing this book. Other than my own memory, she was my major resource for so much of what is contained here. There were times after her passing when I was trying to remember someone's name or a specific date that I would catch myself saying, "I'll ask Mama; she'll know."

For many years my children, Mari and Will, said, "Daddy, you ought to write down these stories so we can read them to our children." So, here they are for Drew and Mia and Lyla and Brynn and all the other people who are now a part of my story.

Table of Contents

PART 3: THE WILD WIND OF ENTERTAINMENT

Introduction

Back some time ago, folks mentioned I ought to write a memoir. They said it was a popular thing for authors to do, and I do enjoy reading about other people's memories. My first reaction was, "I ain't done nothin' worth writin' about." But, like everybody else who gets to the autumn of their life (in my case, it is late autumn), I began to reflect on all I had seen and done, and I still didn't find enough I thought would be of much interest to other folks. However, in the course of reflection, I did remember a lot of interesting people I had met along the way who were, indeed, worth writing about. So, I decided I would write about them instead. After all, Alfred, Lord Tennyson said we are a part of all that we have met. So, I guess this is a kind of memoir.

During my lifetime, I have met a lot of famous people—movie and television stars, and every North Carolina governor since Terry Sanford—but they were not the most important people I met. Some of the people who had the most influence on me were, of course, family members, but beyond them is a wide spectrum of people. I can't include everybody I've ever met in this one volume; there are just too many and, in all honesty, some of them I've tried to forget. I'm sure very few realized, at the time of our acquaintance, that they would have an impact on my life. I can't possibly recall all the details of conversations or specific circumstances of every relationship, so I have taken some "literary liberties" in putting this together.

My goal in writing this is not just to recall encounters I've had with folks but to tell a story about a time and place unique to me: the American South (southeastern North Carolina, in particular) in the second half of the twentieth century and a part of the new millennium. Many of these stories take place in the 1950s, or what I call the Last Golden Age of America, a time of prosperity and optimism for most people and a time when we all seemed to agree on at least one thing: this was the greatest country in the world and nothing was ever going to change that. Personally, so much of the '50s culture was fundamental in forming who I am. But everything turned upside down in the '60s, and the dissolution amplified during the '70s. That idyllic image of our past, now seen through a broken mirror, drove the memories of who we used to be and the good that had existed into such a small part of us that it almost ceased to exist.

I want to paint a picture of what is good about the people I have met and the places I have been.

A regular reader of my columns once chastised me for always painting a beautiful picture of life in "My South." She said, "Life was only good in the South for white males." I'm not naive enough to believe that nothing bad or ugly exists now or even did exist in the place I grew up. However, I still believe I can paint a beautiful picture, warts and all.

I wrote a little poem for a book a did with photographer Doug Sasser. I think it might be a good prelude for this book.

Listen to the South Wind

Listen to the South Wind as it speaks and sings.
It plays its melodies through the pine trees.
It whispers through the coves and screams
through the mountain tops.
It's a voice that ripples over rivers and creeks,
and wanders down dirt roads, and through city streets.

The poet listens to the sound, he soaks in every part,
then writes down all he hears in the corner of his heart.
Hark! The sound of Tarheel voices,
the chant of the auctioneer,
the church choirs singing shaped-note music,
the piano "played by ear."

It wafts 'cross fields of cotton and corn, consoling weary backs,
and lingers in the sawmills where the saw don't cut no slack.
It wraps itself 'round abandoned barns
like kudzu on the run.
Then it changes tone like a fiddler does
with the setting of the sun.
Listen to the South Wind!
It's the sound of you and me,
Of farmers, store clerks,
And those who used to be.

It's the heartbeat of our being,
a plea to keep us free,
for tomorrow comes a-rolling
on each wave that leaves the sea.

I've been riding on the South Wind all my life.

Part 1
THE WARM BREEZE OF FAMILY

The Warm Breeze of Family

Every family has two sides: maternal and paternal. In my case, my maternal side, the Councils, and my paternal side, the Thompsons, were much alike. We all trace our family genes back to England. As in every Southern family, genealogy is important to us. We want to know who we were so we can tell who we are.

So, I want to propose a toast to the current Thompson family, the descendants of Roy Siers Thompson and Clara Powell Thompson. From their union has sprung a unique, complex, diverse group of people defined not only by their individual attributes, but also by the commonality of their diversity. We are a distinctive family that can't be duplicated. Represented in this family is a wide range of personalities with a wide range of talents—not just artistic talents (though that is certainly there) but the talent to accomplish a wide range of worthwhile deeds. We have almost every imaginable occupation represented, and, has always been the case, many of us have more than one occupation or profession and innumerable hobbies. Common amongst us is the tremendous creativity that burst from the minds, souls, and, apparently, the genes of our ancestors.

Many of us have reached out to other gene pools to enrich our own, and these folks have, in turn, added their own talents and attributes to our family. Some of us are fortunate to be born into this family, and others have had the good fortune to join, thereby adding so much to the family. Sarcasm and overstatement are truly defining characteristics in our family, even as we put on that mantle of modesty and decorum.

In my case, I brought two remarkable women to the family. Claudia and I were married for almost twenty-five years, most of them very happy years. In that time we produced two children, Mari and Will. They are our contribution to a continuing family legacy. Whatever failings we may have had, that accomplishment alone overrides our frailties and failures.

Lynda came along in the middle of my life and enhanced it in many ways. She encouraged me not to be "normal." I think I have responded to that encouragement, possibly beyond her intent.

Each year, as we gather to celebrate our family, there are more of us and there are fewer. Each in their own way adds to the value of this family both in their arrival and in their passing. Those who arrive bring a clean slate on which they write and paint their part in our lives, and those who leave bequeath a sprawling picture of who they were and how they affected us. In joining together, we create a vast panorama that will live in our hearts and minds as long as we remember who we are: Roy and Clara's legacy. We are all one family, a small part of the family of God, and we rejoice in the amalgamation.

Here's to the Thompson family, those present, those who have gone before us, and those yet to come—so, we raise our glass to family, long may it live!

The Southern Gentleman

There is a breed of man indigenous to the South, and that breed is fading away even as we speak: the Southern Gentleman. There are other species that seem to have overtaken this old breed, those who have a higher profile in the eye of society. The subsequent diminution in recognition has contributed to the decline of the species. The Good Ol' Boy and even the Redneck are better known—they get more attention in the media.

Still, I believe the Southern Gentleman will endure. The characteristics that have stood him in good stead all these years are characteristics that can survive. Besides, the true Southern Gentleman seems to flourish in his semi-anonymity. Modesty is one of his most apparent characteristics.

The Southern Gentleman may be the last bastion of masculine gentility found anywhere. He abhors the boastful demeanor that so many see as an expression of the male's grasp of his role in society, a role perceived as being just slightly above Cro-Magnon man.

He's as much at home driving a pickup truck as he is behind the wheel of a Cadillac. A Southern Gentleman does not feel the need to make other people aware of his status in society. Instead, he chooses to let his daily interaction with his fellow man speak for him. He appreciates each of his neighbors for their individual attributes, regardless of race, religion, or social background.

There is much of the Renaissance Man in the Southern Gentleman. He has a broad interest in everything around him. He's appreciative and curious about the sciences and the nature of the world. He appreciates both the biological and the aesthetic intricacies that comprise the universe. In many cases, he is a "son of the soil," a man tied to nature for his very existence. Subsequently, he is a religious man who has a strong faith in God and relies on that faith each time he plants his field or his garden. He has a strong affection for God's handiwork, for the ocean, woods, and streams and their inhabitants.

He doesn't confine his athletic pursuits to the cumulative memory of sports statistics, but he appreciates the skill and effort that goes into achieving those statistics. He is aware of the need for the human body to reach and maintain a certain level of fitness, if only for the body to function at its maximum potential.

And when he clothes that body, he does so in a manner that shows his appreciation for tradition and for the dignity that comes from presenting himself well to other people.

A Southern Gentleman appreciates the arts and is involved in some aspect of creativity that allows him to express the beauty of the language or languages we speak, the sights we see, and the sounds we hear. Such an activity is not seen as emasculating but an expression of the God-given talents we all possess.

A Southern Gentleman has an appreciation for education that goes beyond his own personal achievements in that area. He believes education is more than just the accumulation of facts, of information. Education is the ability to use all we have accumulated and process it, to continue to ask questions until we reach our own conclusions through reason.

All of this belies the stereotype of the Southern Gentleman as the master of the manor, content to sit on the veranda of his plantation house, sip bourbon, and talk about race horses. Neither does it portray the scion of "the New South," one whose major role in life is the accumulation of wealth and power. Instead, he can be found most often in the small towns where the quality of life is defined more by the Sunday morning church service than the maneuverings of the boardroom.

These gentlemen are fading away. Each week I am reminded of their passing as I attend more funerals of such men. I am sorry to see them go. We'll probably never see their like again, and we will all be the lesser for it.

The responsibility will fall on those of us left behind, those of us born in a different time and environment, to not merely revere the Southern Gentleman as a memory of a bygone era but to honor his legacy and emulate those characteristics that made him unique.

Daddy

I was talking to a group once up in New Bern, North Carolina, and I told a story about my father, Bill Thompson Sr. In telling the story, I called my father "Daddy." After the program, a gentleman came up and asked if I thought it was appropriate for a sixty-five-year-old man to call his father "Daddy." I told him I thought it was, since that is what I had called him since I was old enough to speak. I didn't tell the gentleman, but I think adult children calling their parents Mama and Daddy may be a Southern thing.

My daddy was a Southern Gentleman. He met all the aforementioned criteria, plus some, and was the most unpretentious man I ever knew. What you saw was what you got. Daddy was a tall, "spare" man who took pride in his health; he never smoked nor drank alcohol. He believed facial hair represented poor hygiene, so he was always clean-shaven, though the hair atop his head was thick and black until it turned shiny and white. His quick step make it seem he was always in a hurry, and in his later years, he developed a small belly that belied his good health. While he was always polite to everyone, you never had to wonder where you stood or what his opinion was. In my daddy's world, there were very few gray areas; there was right and wrong, good and bad, and very little in between.

Daddy was born in Columbus County, North Carolina, in 1922 on a small farm whose main crop was strawberries and, later, tobacco. That

Carolina soil was as much a part of him as it was the fields he worked in. He loved the land. He loved the feel of it, the smell of it, and the sight of it. He was never happier than when he was in those fields.

c⁓

When Daddy was about fifteen years old, his father, my grandfather, had a heat stroke while working in the field. That happened often to those who struggled in the heat of the Carolina summers. So, the field hands working with my grandfather placed him in the back of a mule-drawn wagon to transport him to the cool shade of a barn shelter. In the process, they placed the back of his head in the fork of a wooden cross-bar that held the sides of the wagon together. He recovered from the heat stroke, but the bumping of the wagon and subsequent pounding of that cross-bar on the back of his head created an aneurism that later caused bursts of pain so strong, he would run as fast as he could and as hard as he could, as if he could run away from the pain. My grandfather was a large man; I can imagine how frightening it must have been to watch a man of his size and bulk running out of unknown fear. The frequent attacks caused my Grandfather Roy to leave the farming up to his oldest son. So, at fifteen, my father assumed the head of the farming operation and the care of his family: his mother, sister, and three younger brothers.

Even with all that responsibility, Daddy found time to play baseball. He loved the game almost as much as he loved farming. He played in the old Tobacco State League during his teens and early twenties, right up until he married Mama and she told him he shouldn't be playing ball on Sundays.

The games were played on Sunday afternoons in Whiteville, Kinston, Lumberton, and other small towns in eastern North Carolina. The only thing my daddy loved more than farming and baseball was my mama.

When I was born, Mama and Daddy were living in a renovated tenant house on the farm in Chadbourn. They had done all the work on the old house themselves. Over the years, they added a bedroom, enlarged the kitchen and dining room, added indoor plumbing, and painted the old, weathered gray wood white.

Mama said that before I was born, she would go out at night during tobacco season and stay with Daddy as he tended the old wood-burning tobacco barn curers. Daddy's was a traditional "stick" barn, twenty by sixteen feet wide, and twenty-five feet tall. The wood curer had brick (or perhaps metal) flues that ran around the floor of the barn. The furnace had to be watched carefully through the night and fueled with wood so it wouldn't burn out. It was hard, strenuous work, with very little sleep involved, but Daddy loved it.

In the winter of 1944, the year after I was born, my parents decided to move over to Red Bug, a small community south of Hallsboro. It was near my mother's family, Grandfather Council had just opened a general store, and all the family was joining in to help get the business started. Daddy had planned to return to the farm in Chadbourn in time to plant the spring crop. He told me many years later, that he didn't go back that spring because he knew it had been difficult for Mama to adjust to a farmer's life. The anticipation of the one payday per year, when the crops were sold, was particularly daunting. So, my father stayed and worked in the family business with Mama's family and turned the Thompson family farm operation over to his brother Leroy.

Daddy was in charge of the "outside" operations: fuel and farm supply, sales, and appliance delivery. My Uncle Charles was in charge of "inside," which included a dry-goods grocery (clothes, toys, and such) and the store office. My grandfather was president. My father later became president and held that position until he sold the company and retired in 1987.

It was after Daddy was diagnosed with early-stage Alzheimer's at around eighty years of age that he began to tell me about his youth. That's when he told me about his decision to stay at Council and Company. During that revelatory conversation, I asked him why he'd stayed, knowing how much he had loved farming. He answered, "Sometimes you do things for love you wouldn't do under normal circumstances."

There were a lot of "abnormal" circumstances in Daddy's life. When both my younger sister and I graduated from high school, we went off to college—I to Campbell College and Linda to the University of North Carolina at Chapel Hill. We both received financial assistance from our parents and scholarships. We had both worked during the summers as teenagers and had put our earnings in a savings account to be used for college. But as Linda was just two years younger than me, the cost of both of us in college at the same time exceeded our earnings, plus those or our parents. So, Daddy decided to get another job, not quit the job at Council and Company, but add on an additional job. Somehow, he managed to get a job delivering the mail for the Hallsboro post office. Six days a week, he would get up early in the morning, run that rural mail route in all kinds of weather before noon, and be back at the store to work until dark or later.

"Sometimes you do things for love you wouldn't do under normal circumstances."

My father loved to be around all kinds of people. He loved the people in his community in particular. Sometime in the late 1960s, my father and some other men in the community decided they needed a fire department. So, they organized fundraisers, built a fire station, and bought a fire truck. Those fundraisers and the people from Hallsboro who gave money were from all races, all social classes.

There was a certain invisible and silent dichotomy to the racial interaction in the area where I grew up. Back in the early fifties, a resurgence of the Klu Klux Klan brought national attention to the area. Blatant racism existed in Columbus County. But in Hallsboro, little changed. Maybe it was a feigned amiability, but there was a sense of community between black and white that contradicted the situation elsewhere.

Hallsboro had always been diverse. Blacks and whites worked together at the mills, on the farms, and in the logging woods. There were probably as many black residents as there were white, and we were a very inter-social community—much more than we even realized at the time. There was a separateness, desegregation wouldn't become the law for several more years, but a sense of community seemed to blur that separateness.

When they finally opened the fire station, it was operated by a volunteer fire department made of both men and women, black and white. My daddy was the first fire chief, and Carl Bryant, a black man who ran a used-auto sales and repair shop, was his assistant. After the fire station was built, Daddy and Carl decided to have a community Fourth of July celebration at the station. Everybody brought food and enough sweet tea to satisfy the thirsts of two hundred people. Daddy backed the long bed of his fertilizer truck beside the station to provide a stage. Every church choir, black and white, performed and then everybody sang together in a harmony that sounded beyond the gospel and patriotic songs. Later, they lit a big fireworks show in the field behind the station. And while folks marched in the streets and burned churches across Mississippi and Alabama, the spirit of community settled over all of Hallsboro like a warm blanket that kept out the cold of prejudice. Working together, the town's residents had made a safer place for their families—black and white.

"Sometimes you do things for love you wouldn't do under normal circumstances."

Over the years, I have been honored by different organizations for things I have done. I was inducted into the Order of the Long Leaf Pine, designated a Kentucky Colonel, named Outstanding Young Man of America in 1977 by the American Jaycees, and declared an "honorary citizen" of the states of Texas, Georgia, Florida, Virginia, and Tennessee, as well as numerous cities across the country. I really do appreciate every distinction.

But the greatest honor I've ever received was when somebody told me I reminded them of my daddy.

Aunt Mary Lee and Christmas 1944

Christmas 1944 was not exactly merry for my family, or for most Americans. Our country was in the midst of World War II, though the most immediate concern to my family was the fact that it was raining and cold in southeastern North Carolina. I state this based on my mother's recollection. I was only a little over a year old at the time, so much of what I know of that particular season was told to me over the years. It was to be my first real Christmas.

Like most families during the war, my family had listened carefully to the reports of what was happening in Europe and the South Pacific. They had learned the names of far-away places they had never before heard of, looked them up in the big atlas book of maps, and waited eagerly for the infrequent letters from sons, uncles, and brothers who had been sent to those exotic and dangerous places.

But tradition runs strong in my family, and war or no war, Christmas was a time of celebration. Somehow or other we would recognize the season in as many ways as we could, just as we always had.

One major tradition was finding an appropriate tree to decorate. There aren't a lot of fir trees in this part of the country, so we made do with pine. Those scruffy little trees didn't have the perfect symmetry most associate with Christmas trees. The one my father found for us that year had some uneven gaps between the limbs and wasn't exactly triangular. It more or less resembled a Christmas bush, but it was sufficient for decorating with the limited amount of decorations we had. My mother found some big, long-leaf pine cones and covered them with white flour that looked like snow. She picked up several of the little prickly balls that fell from the sweetgum trees, painted them silver, and draped their long stems across the little pine tree's limbs. She had even saved some of the "icicles," thin streams of tinsel left over from previous years, and placed them gingerly on the tree, then patiently tied tiny red and green ribbon bows to its branches. Of course, the most important element of the tree decoration was the lights. They were big bulbs of red and green. I still believe those are the only true Christmas lights.

The actual celebration of the birth of the Christ child was centered around the church service held at our town's little Baptist church. All the family went to the Christmas Eve service, then returned home and went to bed. That was it. In 1944, I was still the only child, and Santa was not yet a person of my acquaintance, so there was no great anticipation of reindeer and such nor, for a one-year-old baby, much awareness of any of it. But the Thompson tradition of storytelling has passed down the story of that Christmas morning.

My mother, father, and I lived in a small, renovated tenant house on the family farm in Chadbourn. My grandfather and grandmother lived in the "old house" about a hundred yards up the road. That year, we all gathered at my grandparents' for Christmas Day dinner. (Not lunch. Dinner was the noon meal. *Supper* was the evening meal.) After that, we all gathered around the tree in the living room to exchange gifts. My father was the oldest of the five children and the only one married and, of course, I was the only grandchild. The fact I didn't have any idea, about what was going on, the significance of the season, or even who these people were, did not deter my family from making me the center of attention.

My Aunt Mary Lee was just a year younger than my father. She lived and worked in Wilmington, but, like everybody else, she had come home for Christmas. My mother told me Aunt Mary Lee had waited until all the other gifts had been opened to present her special present. She let me tear the wrapping off, but my mother opened the little box that contained the special gift. She removed a large, red glass Christmas tree ball so light and fragile it was almost weightless. It was a wonderful, caring gift. Anything made from glass was very rare during the war. Aware of the fragility of the ornament and the potential danger from the rowdy group, Mama placed it gently back in the box. Later that evening, after we had gone back to our house, Mama took out the Christmas ball, placed it in my little hands, and lifted me up to place the ornament on our shabby tree. Each year thereafter, my mother and I would recreate that special tree-trimming moment (minus the lifting me up part as I got bigger). Later, she would wrap that fragile ornament in tissue paper and store it away until we ceremoniously placed it on the tree at her house each Christmas.

That is until 2017. Time finally caught up with the old ornament as it hung on the tree at Mama's house. The old hanger became detached, causing the ancient glass to fall to the floor and shatter.

An old tradition died, but the spirit of the gift still lives.

Always Get Back On

Almost three-quarters of a century ago, I fell off a horse. The horse was really only a pony, but when you're just five years old, size is irrelevant. It was the first time I'd fallen off a horse, an event that would occur many more times over the years.

Not too long ago, I had another equine altercation. I was riding a very gentle horse, one of several I worked at a farm that belonged to Boys and Girls Homes, when he decided he did not like being saddled or ridden at that particular time. (We discovered later that the poor horse suffered from a stomach ulcer, the pain from which was exacerbated by the tightening of the saddle cinch and my weight in the stirrup.) The moment I placed my foot in the stirrup, he backed up as fast as he could … until he hit an electric fence.

Then it was rodeo time.

I can't say I was thrown from the saddle, since I was never really in it. Most of my short engagement with the saddle involved my tenuous stance in the left stirrup. This experience gave a whole new meaning to "riding side-saddle." So, the horse didn't throw me as much as I made an unconventional exit.

I landed on my chest, resulting in a cracked rib and some bruises. Fortunately, my pride wasn't hurt; there was nobody there to see me as I lay among the dirt and manure of the pasture. Only the small herd of colts on the other side of the fence was witness to my untimely, unplanned, equine-assisted attempt to fly.

I have always believed that when you are thrown from a horse, for whatever reason, you should get back on. So, I walked down the fence line to where the horse stood ever so placidly, got the reins, led him back to the end of the pasture where there was a patch of sand, and remounted. (Actually, *mounted* since I had not completely mounted the first time.) I had sought out the patch of sand in case there was to be a repeat performance. Thankfully, there was no encore, and we went on our way and checked out the status of the newly-arrived herd of cattle in another pasture.

As I rode contentedly through the pastures that afternoon, I recalled other occasions when I had made unplanned departures from the backs of horses. Learning experiences, that's what they were. Although I have suffered the aches and pains, bruises and contusions, and even some broken bones, I don't regret any of it. The pain horses have caused me is greatly out-weighed by the pleasure they have given me over the years.

Oh, and that little pony I rode when I was five was just the beginning. My Uncle Frank (technically my uncle, though just a couple of years older than me) was the instigator of my relationship with horses. That first experience occurred when he led his pony, on which I was astride, across a pasture as we headed back to the barn at my grandmother Thompson's farm. My mother and father walked with us. Of the four humans, Mama was the only one who didn't like horses. Frank, in a playful mood, slipped the halter off the pony, which the pony apparently saw as an opportunity to take off as fast as he could toward the barn, his only encumbrance my excited body clinging to his mane.

I loved it!

But just before we got to the barn, the pony took a sharp turn to the left and deposited my little body a few feet from a hand-dug brick well. To say Mama was not happy is an understatement. Still, after determining I was not injured, my father and Frank insisted I get back on the pony.

That was a valuable lesson learned that day. And I have continued to practice that act of determination seventy years later. You see, a career path can change quickly in the precarious world of television journalism; the matrimonial ride can be rough; and any successful writer must endure hundreds of rejections. I have been through each of those situations, as well as other challenges, and still, I've come out in pretty good shape.

No matter how hard the fall, I always got up and tried again.

Frank and the Chickens in the Well

From the time I was about five years old until I was about fifteen, I spent the summers with my Grandmother Thompson. Since we were so close in age, my Uncle Frank was the closest thing I ever had to a brother and we shared many adventures. Many of them included Frank rescuing me from predicaments I had gotten myself into.

I had the usual curiosity of a six-year-old boy, and the farm presented many questions for my inquisitive mind. For instance, "Can chickens swim?" I had seen ducks swimming in the ponds, and they looked kinda like chickens. They had feathers and wings.

So, to answer my question, I decided to conduct an experiment. After considerable effort, I rounded up some chickens in the pen next to the barn. Catching the individual chickens was not easy. They were what we now refer to as "free-range" chickens, not used to any form of confinement. They were healthy and excitable, but I succeeded in catching two of them and tossing them down my grandmother's hand-dug well.

It did not take long for me to determine that chickens could not swim, and afterward, it didn't occur to me that two dead chickens would pose any kind of problem to our household's primary source of water. When my grandmother got home and discovered the result of my experiment, she was not happy. She tore off a "switch"—a long, thin branch from a bush next to the back porch—and proceeded to inflict justified punishment on my body.

As Grandmama was completing her punishment, Frank came to the backyard from the tobacco field, having heard my cries for mercy. He tried to explain to Grandma how I hadn't known any better, but she maintained that I had *learned* better. Her main concern was not my physical condition at that time but, rather, the contaminated well water. She told Frank and me to get the dead chickens out of the well right then, explaining how it would take days for the well to de-contaminate itself.

After some discussion, Frank and I decided he would tie a rope around my chest, lower me into the well, and then bring me back up with the two chickens. Fortunately, Frank was big and strong and I was small, but he did strain a little. Despite the heat of the Carolina summer, the water was *cold*. And have you ever smelled wet, dead chickens? I got the two malodorous birds and then Frank pulled me out of the well. In my youthful ignorance, I asked Frank if he thought Grandmama would fry the dead chickens. He told me I would be lucky if she didn't fry me.

Frank (I never called him "Uncle Frank") was my hero then and still is. The term "hero" is often misused today. So, I looked up the word in the dictionary just to make sure I had it right in my own mind. According to *Merriam-Webster's Collegiate Dictionary*, a hero is "a man admired for his achievements and noble qualities," "the central figure in an event, period, or movement," "an object of extreme adoration or devotion." It was a confirmation of what I already knew: my uncle/brother, Frank Thompson, was a hero. I'd known it all along.

Frank became a hero to me when I was just a little boy. Frank was only a few years older than me and I was his opposite: I was little and he was big. He could already ride a horse by himself and I still needed some help. Frank could hit a baseball out of the park and I could barely swing the bat. He could crop a row of tobacco and I had to pick up the leaves around the barn. He even knew how to hitch a mule to a drag and ride on the drag while standing. I had to ride behind the hames on the mule's back. But Frank taught me how to do each of those things (except hitting the baseball out of the park, that was all Frank). These things may seem insignificant, but to a little boy growing up during the 1950s in southeastern North Carolina, they were all really important.

As we got older, Frank drove a car before I did. Still, he taught me how to drive a tractor, then let me drive his car before I got my license … even after I'd run it into a crepe myrtle tree. He graduated from high school and college before I did. I went with Daddy and my uncles and grandmother to just about every football game Frank played at Wake Forest—home and away. He was co-captain of the team. He dated girls before I did and got married before I did, though I was in his wedding and he was in mine. He even had children before I did. I watched how well Frank accomplished each new endeavor and learned from him. He was that "object of extreme adoration and devotion." Plainly spoken, I wanted to be like Frank.

As I got older, Frank became more than just a central figure in events. I began to admire him not only for his achievements but for his noble and heroic characteristics. He showed me how to treat people and to appreciate them regardless of their social status, while at the same time talking and interacting with them as equals. He taught me that people in corporate board rooms and people working in fields were due the same respect, and how I was also their equal.

I always thought being a hero must've been easy for Frank. He wasn't called "Big Frank" just for his size. He had a big heart and a big personality that drew people to him. I was a little nerd with glasses and buck teeth. Frank was the epitome of athletic beauty: rugged and tall with a smile that lit up his face. I was nothing like him, but he told me I could do anything I set my mind to—and I took his advice.

Of all the things Frank taught me, probably the most significant is how family is so important in life. We don't get to pick our families. We don't get to choose the ones we want to keep and the ones we don't. We are all family all the time, through good and bad times, in triumph and tragedy, in sickness and health. You gotta love 'em all unconditionally. Just like Frank did.

Some folks are bigger than life. They exude a presence wherever they are that sweeps people up, makes them feel good just wherever that person is. Frank was always like that. But Frank is bigger than death too. Just because his body has left this earth, doesn't mean he isn't still here. He will always be here as long as we remember him.

Some time ago Frank, his wife Betty, and I were sitting in their house in Sanford, talking about the old days on the farm in Chadbourn and the things the family did back then. Frank said, "You make sure everybody [meaning the family] knows this stuff we've been talking about so they'll know where they came from and who we are." So, that's what I'm doing: sharing our stories and remembering Frank, because he was a big part of who we are.

And he's still my hero.

Leroy

The warehouse was hot. Even the breeze that blew through the several wide doors was hot. Dust from the concrete floor and from the piles of cured tobacco floated in the streaks of sunlight that trickled through the skylights. Above it all resonated the melodic, mystical chant of the auctioneer as he led a line of buyers and ticket markers and sellers and onlookers through the long, golden-hued piles of tobacco. In the midst of that line was a man who walked awkwardly, using his hips to move his legs, exerting tremendous energy to propel himself through the heat and the dust and never slow down the procession. He never asked for any accommodation; he sweated in the heat just like everybody else. To him, and everybody in that warehouse, the tobacco market was not just the economic engine of southeastern North Carolina in the twentieth century, it was the keystone of a culture, a way of life that would eventually disappear and become only a memory.

My uncle, Leroy Thompson, was not only a product of Southern culture during the early twentieth century, he helped create it. He was born and raised on a tobacco farm, and it was central to his life. He had grown, harvested, and sold tobacco since childhood. He became a bookkeeper and a buyer for a national tobacco company, and he eventually owned his own warehouse, where he held a market to auction and sell the crop. Anybody who took on the challenge of such a demanding way of life needed to be determined, persistent, and have a clear understanding of what was needed to be successful. In Leroy's case, the challenge was even greater: he had been crippled by a rabid dog bite when he was just a small boy.

As a child, I never really took Leroy's physical condition into consideration. He, like my uncle Frank, was only a few years older than me, and his physical situation never kept him from doing anything the rest of us did. He rode horses, played baseball in the front yard, worked in the fields, drove a tractor, went to school, dated girls, eventually got married and raised a family.

Leroy was the brother who was most directly involved in the operation of the family farm. After my father moved to Hallsboro and Leroy's older brother, my Uncle Lacy, went to work with the funeral home in Chadbourn, Leroy and Frank, still in high school, remained to work under Grandma Thompson's tutelage.

Later on, Leroy went to business school before beginning work as a bookkeeper with a tobacco company. Eventually, he bought his own warehouse, having secured several investors and a considerable loan from the bank, all the while continuing to operate the family farm.

Leroy's attitude about his inability to walk like everybody else was not so much a denial of the condition but denying that condition the ability to define who he was. How he walked, or even the fact that he walked at all, did not define him. After people got to know him, they never thought about his physical condition. The challenge of walking didn't form his personality.

⁓

One summer when I was about fourteen, Leroy decided to expand the farm operation to include cucumbers. There was a produce market there in Chadbourn, which made selling cucumbers easy. Growing cucumbers in the sandy soil was relatively easy. But the harvesting was a difficult task.

Cucumbers grow on vines that spread across the ground; they don't climb a stalk. That means in order to harvest said vegetable, a harvester must bend over—in the oppressive heat of the Carolina summer in this case—pull each cucumber from the vine, and deposit them in a container. Harvesting was my role that summer. I had "cropped" tobacco (pulled the leaves from the stalk) and picked corn, both physically demanding jobs, but they were light work compared to harvesting cucumbers.

Everyone knew that when you worked with Leroy, you didn't complain. It was simply not done, partly because it didn't accomplish anything, but mostly because everybody was in the same situation. All of the field hands, including my cousins and me, worked in the same fields under the same conditions: hot, sandy, back-breaking work. But the main reason we didn't complain was because Leroy worked the same fields and did the same work we did.

However, teenage boys are known for not always being sensitive to situations. On one particularly hot day in the cucumber field, I told Leroy he wasn't paying me enough to work in such conditions. So, he said he'd pay me an extra dollar for every fifty-pound sack of cucumbers I picked that was more than he picked. I took him up on the deal. Within a couple of hours, I was behind by four sacks of cucumbers.

⌒

As I was growing up, Frank and Leroy were more like my brothers than my uncles. Even when we were grown, that was still the case. Later, during the 1970s and '80s when I emceed pageants and festivals all over the country, Leroy would often loan me his cars, and they were nice. I remember a Thunderbird he loaned me to drive down to the Beaufort Water Festival in South Carolina. It was a luxury car, complete with a CB radio, leather seats, an 8-track tape player, and a sunroof.

As I left Columbia headed to Beaufort, I called on the radio to ask for any evidence of "smokies" (highway patrol officers) down the road. I got a reply saying the road was clear. Thus encouraged, I set the cruise control to eighty-five miles an hour in the sixty-mile-an-hour zone. In just a few minutes, a blue light flashed in my mirror and I pulled over.

The patrolman gave me an option: I could take the ticket and come back to court at a later date, or I could plead guilty, sign a form to that effect, and pay him right then. I asked how much the fine was and was told it was one hundred dollars. I told the officer I didn't have that much cash. He asked how much I had, and I told him: sixty dollars. He said that would do, and I thought that would be the end of the incident.

However, a couple of months later, Leroy told me his auto insurance company had raised his insurance premium because of a ticket issued in South Carolina. He said I could pay him the amount of the premium or help him pick cucumbers that season.

… I paid the premium.

The Governor, a Balogna Sandwich, and the President of the United States

*P*olitics was always a part of my family on both sides. My uncles, Charles Council and Lacy Thompson, were both Columbus county commissioners during the '50s and '60s, and served together for part of that time. Uncle Lacy was the Columbus county clerk of court for over thirty years. Both were Democrats at a time when the party concept was merely theoretical in North Carolina, and throughout much of the South. My Grandfather Council had been an unsuccessful candidate for district judge.

I may be a little less then objective when I say my family looked at politics as public service. Many of my Sunday afternoons were spent out at my Grandfather Council's house in Red Bug, listening to him, my uncles, and my father talk about politics. From when I was about seven years old in the early 1950s until I graduated from college in 1965, they taught me a lot about how the US government works. I also learned that politics is a personal thing, no matter how politicians might try to dress it up with philosophy. Every candidate has a personal agenda. However, I do remember my grandfather saying on one of those Sunday afternoons, "Boys, if you don't remember who voted you into office, you'll only serve one term."

c⁓

When Uncle Charles was a county commissioner, there was a steady stream of folks coming and going to the family store in Hallsboro. Some wanted political favors and some just wanted to complain. The political traffic got so bad in there, my grandfather forbade political discussions on the store's property. Some of the exchanges would get kinda rowdy, with heated language and the occasional fistfight. My grandfather said it kept out the paying customers. However, since it was almost impossible to follow Granddaddy's edict, Uncle Charles would invite visitors to his office at the back of the store.

One day in the summer of 1964, when I was just nineteen years old, we had a special visitor. Uncle Charles was chairman of the Democratic party in the county and a delegate to the upcoming Democratic national convention. On that rainy day, Governor Terry Sanford made an unannounced visit to the store. (At least, it was unannounced to everybody except Uncle Charles.) The governor had called my uncle the night before to say he would be making a visit to Boys Home at Lake Waccamaw (now Boys and Girls Homes of North Carolina) the next day, and he needed to talk with Uncle Charles while he was in the area.

About noon, the governor and three other fellas pulled up to the store. The highway patrol escort that had accompanied Governor Sanford to Boys Home continued on to Whiteville, giving the impression to the press that the governor would be heading there as well.

My family members and I were genuinely surprised to see the governor of North Carolina come into our little store as nonchalantly as any local customer. I was introduced to Mr. Sanford and then instructed by Uncle Charles to lock the front door. After doing as I was told, I looked around for Uncle Charles and the governor, thinking they had retreated to the back office. Instead, I saw that the whole entourage, our family as well as the governor and his friends, had gone to the meat market area of the store.

Our store, Council and Company, had one of the most modern custom meat markets for its time, but I never thought of it as a showpiece. We bought whole carcasses of beef and pork and customized the cuts for each customer. I soon learned, however, that Uncle Charles wasn't concerned with showing off the meat market. Rather, it was to be the site of an impromptu luncheon.

My father stood behind the meat counter, cutting slices of bologna and cooked ham. My mother took those slices and made fresh sandwiches for everybody. Uncle Charles told me to fetch a bunch of cold Pepsis out of the water cooler at the front of the store, then I joined my mother, father, and Aunt Lucile where they stood at one end of the meat market, while my uncle and the governor stood and talked politics at the other. In particular, they discussed the national convention for which Uncle Charles and Governor Sanford were delegates. There had been some talk of our governor becoming the vice-presidential candidate to replace Lyndon Johnson on the ticket with John Kennedy, but that had all changed with the assassination of President Kennedy.

That tableau in the meat market sticks in my mind to this day: the chief executive of the state of North Carolina sharing a meal in our small country store. At the time, I think I was just impressed at meeting a celebrity; but now, after a lifetime of meeting celebrities, I may be a little jaded about the "celebrity" part. What impresses me as I reflect back on that day is the egalitarian image of a national leader conferring with ordinary citizens about the future direction of the country. My grandfather Council had died the previous year, but I realize now how proud he, the descendent of immigrants, would have been to have his store host such an event.

⌒

Years later, in 1979, I was working at Campbell University as director of corporate and foundation relations when Dr. Norman Wiggins, president of the university, called me and told me he wanted me to accompany him to a symposium on public funding for private education to be held at Duke University.

It wasn't very far from the Campbell campus in Buies Creek to Durham. There was a reception to be held on the Duke campus the night before the symposium. I went with Dr. Wiggins and some other staff members to the event. There was a formal receiving line where former Governor Sanford, then president of Duke University, greeted each of us. When I introduced myself to President Sanford, I just couldn't resist bringing up our chance meeting from so many years before when he had joined us for lunch in the back of that little country store in Hallsboro. When I asked if he remembered the occasion, he laughed and said, "It was the best balogna sandwich I ever had." He then asked about Uncle Charles and the rest of the family.

I thought that was remarkable—that a man of such standing who had met so many people in his life would still remember a relatively insignificant event. But he must have; I'd never mentioned Uncle Charles's name when I brought it up in the receiving line. But Mr. Sanford did. That was the kind of thing that made him such a successful politician.

You gotta vote for a man who likes balogna sandwiches.

⌒

In the fall of 1964, when I was still a student at Campbell University and had just returned from summer break, I joined the staff of the student newspaper, *The Creek Pebbles*. President Lyndon Johnson had succeeded to the presidency of the United States following the death of President John Kennedy. President Johnson was to make a stop at Reynolds

Coliseum in Raleigh that fall as part of his campaign for the election to the office. As part of the press, our staff figured we should be there. The fact that we were not "official" press never entered our minds.

There were four of us: Dave Stevens, my roommate and our editor; Nancy McLaughlin, staff reporter and Dave's girlfriend (whom he would marry and later divorce); Macy Hoyle, our photographer; and me. We had not consulted with our faculty advisor or anybody connected with the college before deciding to cover President Johnson's visit. We were the "free" press and, thus, beyond the constraints of anybody. Relishing in our freedom, we typed up our own press credentials and went to Raleigh.

When we got to Reynolds Coliseum, the crowd was tremendous. Undeterred and still naively optimistic, we presented our credentials to the folks at the door marked "PRESS ONLY." The man at the door looked at Dave's "credentials" and laughed. "Forget it, guys. This is for the real press." Even as Dave protested that we *were* the real press, we knew we were not going in that door.

Nancy was the quintessential, perky, never-say-die optimist. She was also beautiful. Her nickname on campus was "Alice in Wonderland" because she had beautiful, long, curly, blond hair, and she was always so exuberant. She knew everybody on campus and, as we were to find out, a lot of people off campus.

"Come on," she said. "We'll get in." So, we followed Nancy around to the back of the coliseum where we were told the president would arrive. As soon as we got there, Nancy said, "Come on. I know how we can get in."

We nudged our way through the crowd to where a truck was parked and people were unloading musical instruments and sound equipment. Immediately, Nancy rushed over to one of the crew and talked to him, then motioned for us to join her. It seemed Nancy knew members of the band that was playing for the event prior to Mr. Johnson's speech. She handed each of us a musical instrument to carry. I was given a guitar case. As the crew member walked ahead of us, pushing a large speaker on a hand truck, we followed him right into the auditorium and onto the stage.

What luck! we thought. It never occurred to us that we had just bypassed national security that was set up to prevent anyone from posing a threat to the president of the United States. This was less than a year after President Kennedy had been assassinated. In retrospect, I don't know if we were innocent or just stupid.

As we helped the band set up, I saw a familiar figure across the stage. Congressman Alton Lennon, the representative from my district, was talking to some men near the podium. I thought it perfectly natural to walk over and talk to him. He was a frequent visitor to the store at Hallsboro.

As I walked toward him, he recognized me and said, "William, what are you doing here?" I told him I was representing my school paper. He asked how I had gotten on stage, and I told him. He immediately grabbed my arm and pulled me over to the side of the stage. "You can get in a lot of trouble for this," he said. I could tell he was not happy to see me. He reached inside his coat pocket and pulled out a sheet of small yellow decals. He said, "Put this on where it can be seen." Then he gave me three more for my cohorts. "This will keep you out of trouble for a while, but as soon as the president gets here, you need to get out of here." I gave the little stickers to my friends, and we decided we'd wait by the doorway, so that as soon as we had seen the president, we could get out quickly.

In a short while, President Johnson arrived. He was escorted by a big entourage of secret service men and politicians. Macy started taking pictures, which didn't seem out of the ordinary, so nobody noticed us as we eased our way toward the big door that opened up to the coliseum's loading dock. President Johnson was taking his time coming in, shaking hands with everybody. Dave, Nancy, and I wanted our picture taken with the president, so we stood and waited where we knew he would pass. As he reached us, he shook hands with us without even looking and then proceeded on into the coliseum.

In the hustle and bustle, Macy had missed the picture.

On the way back to Buies Creek, we discussed how we would handle our situation with our advisor Mr. Kennedy, and President Campbell. On the one hand, we had shaken hands with the President of the United States. On the other hand, we'd almost gotten ourselves arrested. We didn't know at the time that Macy had failed to get the photo of us with the president. The next day, when Macy told us there was no photo, we made the unanimous decision to not say a word about our trip.

Still, we had memories that would last our lifetimes.

Then There Was Uncle Lacy

Sometimes a man comes along who wittingly or unwittingly defines his generation: a man born in the early years of the most exciting century in history, who survived the struggles of the Great Depression while tending his farm, served his country in the military, overcame personal challenges that would whip other people, and achieved a record of unparalleled service to his community, and persevered to build a life for his family. That was my Uncle Lacy Thompson.

Oh my, how he loved life! Like the sweet tea he adored, he drank life down in great enthusiastic gulps and then sipped and savored its sweetness a little bit at a time.

Uncle Lacy never met a stranger. As soon as he met someone, that person became a friend. While aware of their virtues and foibles, their tragedies and triumphs, and regardless of race, religion or social standing: he treated everyone the same. In nearly a half-century of elective office, first as a county commissioner, then as county clerk of court, he never lost an election. When asked once how he'd accomplished that, he said, "I never quit running when the election was over. I never forgot who got me elected."

Uncle Lacy was always ready to help folks who came to him seeking some kind of assistance. He always did what he could. One of my cousins took a speeding ticket to Uncle Lacy when he was was clerk of court, asking,

"What can we do about this?" Uncle Lacy's answer to his nephew was as straight forward and honest as it was to anyone else: "Pay it."

Uncle Lacy took an unusual route to public service. He was very young when his father (my grandfather) had suffered the stroke, so he went to live with a gentleman named Mr. A.D. Peacock and his family in Chadbourn. (Mr. Peacock later founded Boys Home at Lake Waccamaw.) The Peacocks owned and operated a funeral home. Over the course of time, young Lacy would attend Gupton School of Mortuary down in Georgia and become a licensed mortician who worked in Mr. Peacock's funeral business.

In those days before rescue squads, funeral homes provided emergency ambulances for occasions that required such a service. A hearse may have doubled as an ambulance back then (though, I always thought that such substitution was, at the least, disconcerting to an injured person). Such activities brought Uncle Lacy into contact with law enforcement and the local legal profession. So, when the occasion arose that there was to be an election for county coroner, Uncle Lacy used his contacts and experience with handling bodies—both injured and deceased—as a qualification for office. He won handily. Later he used that political experience to be elected to the office of county commissioner, and finally to run for the office of clerk of court, which he also won and held for over thirty years until his retirement.

C～

Like so many Southern Gentlemen of his time, Uncle Lacy had a certain tie to the land. That tie was evidenced by his joy in planting and working his garden, always planting enough vegetables to share with everybody in the county. He had a faith rooted in God that made him believe those seeds would grow. And as he worked with the people of his county, he was mindful of their ties to the land as well. He knew how families felt about the legacy left to them. Much of Columbus County was and is farming country. Almost every family had a "family farm" that was handed down from generation to generation. As clerk of court, Uncle Lacy was involved in every transfer of family property, and he made every effort to see that families held on to their heritage. Still, this was not an easy task and, as a result, he was not always popular.

⌐⌐

Uncle Lacy took great pride in his family, rejoiced in our accomplishments, and was never shy about telling everybody about us. He was at every graduation ceremony for each of his nieces and nephews, and attended all of Frank's high school and college ball games. He was a great one for calling us every time we made the honor roll, were named all-conference, or got some sort of recognition in the newspaper.

No matter where he went, Uncle Lacy knew everybody and everybody knew him. If you traveled to any place in North Carolina and let people know you were from Columbus County, they'd surely ask, "Do you know Lacy Thompson?"

Some might say pride is not a virtue, but I believe the pride Uncle Lacy had in his family—that large, sometimes rowdy, always loving family of his wife, sons, daughters, grandchildren, great-grand-children, great-great grandchildren, brothers, sisters, nieces and nephews, all the in-laws, and all the extended family—the pride he had in what he was able to do for his community; and his unwavering commitment to his church; was all due to the caring spirit that identified him. That same spirit had made him who he was: a loving, compassionate man I was pleased to call my uncle.

To refer to Genesis and borrow loosely from the poet, James Weldon Johnson:

"And God looked down on all that he had made … including Lacy Randolph Thompson … and said, 'That's Good!'"

The Old House in the Field

I have to be careful where I put my feet on this narrow, worn, and muddy road that leads to the Old Place, my mama's birthplace. Although there is a deep, slit of a ditch on each side of the road, the morning shower has left the grown-over, two-rutted road just wet enough to make it difficult not to get my shoes muddy.

The ditches drain the woods on one side of the road and a wide, un-planted field on the other. On the wooded side runs the remains of an old, barbed-wire fence. The sagging wire lays on the ground among the weeds, until it emerges at irregular intervals to cling to old cedar posts that still stand defiantly where they were placed many years ago, silently challenging the ravages of time and the elements that wear them away.

The big, dormant field stretches almost to the western horizon where the late afternoon sun hangs reluctantly, delaying its descent into the chill of the autumn night. The soybeans that covered its expanse all summer have now been harvested and the old plants plowed under. I can still smell the newly-tilled earth, the musky-sweet scent amplified by the wetness of the rain, the perfume that tempts nature to keep its promise of spring, even as the cold winter winds try to blow it away.

The broom straw and grass on the old road waves slowly as the silent breeze deftly laps at it. It ebbs just enough to assure me that its brown color merely hides life below the surface; soon it will burst into bright green come spring. A bird hops about, rustling fallen leaves just enough to prevent the silence from overwhelming my senses.

⌒

At the end of the old road lies all that's left of a wooden gate, the last remnant of a fence that once surrounded the old house. The house itself sits gray now, like an old man ravaged by time yet still a little rebellious, hanging on to the last vestige of dignity, insolent in the face of age. The windows are boarded up, the porch sags, and several boards are missing. The old brick steps are still there, the most insubordinate element, the part of the house that has changed the least. The brick chimney that once jutted straight up from the living room and through the middle of the house has been decapitated; its loose bricks cleave to the roof, refusing to slide any farther. The kitchen chimney stands stoically, however, every brick in place.

The house doesn't look forlorn, maybe just a little decrepit. Maybe that's because it is surrounded by old trees, friends that have been there almost as long as the house has. The trees are still sturdy. Even in the late fall, their leaves cling to the old limbs that cast long, wide shadows in the afternoon light.

I don't know if it is by design or just circumstance that each tree is a different variety. There is one oak, one pine, one sweetgum, one dogwood, and one pecan.

The dogwood is the most barren, its leaves having departed with the first frost. It stands closest to the house, just a few steps from the dogtrot that separates the kitchen from the rest of the home.

The sweetgum seems to emulate the house, taking pride in its sturdiness and distaining any implication that it might not be as regal as the monumental oak that rises a few feet from it. The gum tree still has some green leaves, while all of the oak's remaining leaves have turned to red and gold.

The pine tree is the largest of the five, proclaiming its monarchy by extending its green boughs regally over the tops of the other trees.

⁓

The pecan tree stands on the east side of the house, some distance from the other trees. Several limbs are scattered on the ground. As I walk over to it, I notice there are already pecans on the tree, some bursting out of their greenish-black hulls, some with their hulls hugging them tight like mothers reluctant to let their children go. There are also nuts strewn across the ground, a few still attached to fallen limbs. I pick up a couple, crack them in my hand, and begin to pick the shells away from the fruit inside. How many times in my life have I done that: picked up pecans from this very ground, placed them in tin buckets, and taken them to my grandmother who baked them into delicious pies?

This was my mother and grandmother's birthplace. It was built by my great-grandfather shortly after the Civil War, a small board-and-batten structure that served the family through three generations. I never really knew my great-grandfather. He died shortly after I was born. But some folks say he was "a tough old codger."

Kinda like his land and the house he built. Mama's house.

There's a place not far from here where people seldom go,
a place that's never seen the light of the neon glow.
'Bout the only way you can get there now
is to get old folks to show you how.

In a time long ago, there was a small farm
where a family lived safe, hidden from harm.
With a mule, a cow, some pigs, and a dog or two,
three sons and two daughters 'fore they were through.

The wife kept house plus a whole lot more
while the father took care of a country store.
They all stayed busy, never got bored,
and only asked for help from the Lord.

As time went on each left that place,
packed their bags and turned their face
toward lives of hope and joy and things,
sharing a bond only family brings.

Now the "Old Place" is gone, fire didn't leave much,
just memories of good times and love and such.
But some thoughts never leave, 'gives our hearts a tug,
when we think 'bout how things were back in Red Bug.

POEM BY MILDRED THOMPSON

I Remember Mama

The room is spartan: just a couple of chairs, a small table, a closet, and a floor lamp beside the bed. But there are lots of pictures of family on every available surface. Mama looks fragile, though she is very much aware of her appearance. On Thursdays, she gets her hair done, regardless of any other activity.

As I write this, my mother, Mildred Council Thompson, is living in a nursing home. She is ninety-three years old. I go to see her every day, sometimes twice a day. She can't get up out of her bed for very long, but she is usually alert and wants to know how all the family is doing. I go through the list: each of her children, grandchildren, and great-grandchildren, citing all of their respective good and bad events. On Sundays, she wants to know how many people were at church and what the preacher's sermon was about. Then she wants to know what I'm going to be doing the rest of the week. After I tell her all that, I ask her if she needs anything, to which she always replies, "Y'all [our family] are everything I need." Then, as I start to leave she always says, "You be a good boy now, ya hear?"

She has given me that same instruction since I was first old enough to leave the house without her. Unfortunately, I haven't always followed her instructions. Even then, she was always there to rescue me, to salvage me, to support me, and to remind me that I "knew better" than to get into whatever mishap had occurred.

By now, almost everybody has heard the term "Steel Magnolia" applied to Southern women. *Sometimes* I think Mama meets the criteria of that floral standard applied to strong women who still cherish the rules of society and value civility. They require a certain level of social conduct that is dignified and refined, that reflects good taste but is underlined by an inner spirit of strength that comes from "good raising." Mama is strong on the good raising, though she may waver in some other aspects.

Mama gave my sister and me etiquette lessons when we were children. Sunday dinner at home was the venue for such instruction. She said we would need to know all the proper ways to conduct ourselves as we went out into the world. "I don't want you to look like country come to town," she said. But then she also said, "Don't forget who you are and where you came from."

Mama and Daddy got married in Dillon, South Carolina, when Mama was just seventeen years old. I asked my father what my Grandfather Council had said when he and Mama told him they were married. "Nothing," Daddy answered, "for about a month."

Back then married girls didn't go back to school, so Mama never finished high school, but she still put a high value on education. My sister and I never doubted that we would someday go to college. Mama said we would and that made it so.

Mama instilled in us a love of reading. I was about ten years old when she bought a set of encyclopedias from a traveling salesman, and paid for them on a time payment plan. I remember how most of that summer, my sister and I lay on the floor of our screened-in porch, reading every volume of that set of encyclopedias.

Our small porch was attached to the north side of the house, so it caught a nice breeze in the summer. It was screened top to bottom on three sides, with a door that opened to the outside in case we wanted to let the dog in. There was a short wicker sofa off to one side, though we preferred the sturdy wooden floor that cooled our lightly-clothed bodies as we lay prone to read.

In our little rural community, the bookmobile came once a month during the summer and parked down at the post office. My sister and I always went. Mama would tell us to take our Radio Flyer wagon and we'd load that wagon with stories of faraway places, famous people, and adventure beyond our town. Mama said getting books was like ordering food in a restaurant; we could get all we wanted, but we had to consume all we got.

It wasn't until Mama had to move to the nursing home that we found out how, in addition to reading (she read about four books a week, delivered to her by the county library), she also loved to write. We found stacks of yellow legal pads and composition books full of stories she had written, as well as several poems. When we asked her about them, she brushed us off, saying, "Oh, that's just some stuff I wrote when the notion struck me." She had thrown away a lot of her musings before we were aware of them, but we were able to save some. Mama has always been so proud of the books and other things I've written, but she was no prouder nor more pleased than I was to find her writings.

The first book I wrote, *Sweet Tea, Fried Chicken, and Lazy Dogs*, was dedicated to my mother and father. As I was writing my first novel, *Celia Whitfield's Boy*, Mama gave me a lot of information about the 1920s, the time period of the story. Part of the story involved a romance between the main character, Jacob Whitfield, and a girl who had come back to his home town. My editor at that time suggested I be a little more graphic in describing the love scenes between Jacob and the girl. "People expect that nowadays," he said. I usually follow the advice of my editors, but in this case, after careful consideration, I decided to keep the book G-rated. I decided I would never write anything that would be embarrassing for my mother to read, particularly when I *knew* she was going read it. I still adhere to that standard, even though I know she may not read it now.

One reason I'm not completely sure the Steel Magnolia title can be applied to Mama is the fact that she was never the society matron who gave lavish parties or wore expensive clothes in the latest style, nor did she ever consider trying to fit into a group where that sort of thinking was part of the mindset. Mama often said she was just a country girl. "That's what your daddy married, that's what he got, and that's what I am," she said. Still, that did not deter her from keeping the cleanest house in the world. Daddy once said, "We could eat off Mildred's floor if it wasn't so uncomfortable."

Mama liked everything to be in its proper place, both at home and in life. She didn't think you should applaud for anything during a church service, and you always wore your best clothes to church. ("God expects you to bring your best to His house.")

For most of her life, Mama worked in the family store there in Hallsboro. She worked there every day, even when my sister and I were going to school. She thought it her duty to work with her husband and support the family. So, she worked during the day, then came home and cleaned her house, fed the family, and made sure we all went to church on Sunday. She even taught Sunday school and sang in the choir.

On reflection, I don't think Mama is so much a Steel Magnolia as an Iron Azalea; she is her own unique species, beautiful and everlasting.

A Walk for Ice Cream

It was a cold, gray spring morning; the kind of morning that makes you want to wiggle down into the covers of the bed and hide from the dismal pledge of the cloudy sky. But I overcame the pull of that self-indulgence and plunged through a Saturday of household chores I had put off all week. Well, maybe more than a week. My wife had said we needed to begin the annual spring-cleaning ritual, at least the indoor portion that involved cleaning out closets.

As usual, I acquiesced to her stringent urging (*some would say nagging, but not I, dear*) and applied myself to the job at hand throughout the morning. Happily, just as we sat down to lunch, my daughter and granddaughter arrived for an afternoon visit. After we had all eaten lunch, my granddaughter announced she wanted to "help Granddaddy." Sounded good to me.

A few minutes after my granddaughter and I began our work, we decided we had really earned a break. I knew that meant a trip to Pierce and Company, the general store less than a mile down the road from the house. They sell ice cream unlike the ordinary brands stored in our kitchen freezer; it is special. But you have to go there to experience it.

As if on cue or, perhaps, at the direction of my granddaughter, the dark clouds that had hung around all morning gave way to sunshine as we left the house and headed down the way to Pierce and Company.

There are few things that compare to the feel of sunshine as it touches a body grown accustomed to winter's cool, damp air, but the touch of a small child's hand in yours is matchless. I relished those two feelings as we set off toward the store.

I felt almost euphoric as we walked across the lawn. The faint smell of rain still lingered as just the slightest breeze stirred the small blades of green grass that emerged through the brown sepulcher of winter. Our feet sank into the soft wetness of the earth, raising pools of water that had just recently descended from the clouds.

There's a long, white fence that leaves the edge of our property and separates a pasture from the road that leads to the store. Horses used to graze there, but now there is only an old barn. The rusted and torn remnants of its tin roof blew in the easy breeze that day, as the sun caught the movement that bounced its light like fairy dust across the roof and through the pecan trees before sprinkling it over the barn.

"Look, Granddaddy!" my granddaughter piped. A white heron had emerged slowly from the edge of the woods that lined the road. The gangly, elegant bird lifted its skinny legs in exaggerated steps, its long neck darting into the water that had slipped the banks of the ditch that ran along the road and merged with the flooded stand of pine and sweetgum trees.

As we watched the bird, I noted a distinctive smell of wet leaves and pine straw. Some arboreal detritus had been shifted from the floor of the woods to the edge of the road as the water had risen then receded, leaving a wavy, embroidered, brown edge between the road and the ditch.

Just beyond the woods before the store sits an old church. Built back in the late nineteenth century, its religious services have ceased, but the building has served many purposes over the years: a library, a club house, a Boy Scout hut, and a hut for VFWs. Now it sits abandoned, though I keep the yard mowed out of loyalty. It's where my family went to church before a new one was built just down the road apiece around 1930. The old church's white paint has begun to fade again, but its long-paned windows are still intact, and the structure is still sturdy—just like the people who built it. Our people.

Not a car had passed since my granddaughter and I left the house, so the sudden swish of water and rush of wind from a passing truck startled both of us, and I felt the squeeze of her little hand. I liked that.

We entered Pierce and Company through the side door (actually the main entrance), and I was immediately swept back in time as I always am when I visit the old store. I have often recounted the mystical transformation of time that occurs in that place. Of course, we got the ice cream immediately; but while we were eating it, I strolled through the gardening section, thinking about what my wife and I would plant for our spring garden. There is a special feeling that goes through a body as you sift seeds through your hands, as you lift small bundles of potted plants and feel the soil around them.

It's like you're feeling life itself.

We finished our ice cream and headed home. As we got out the door of the store, the rain began to fall, first slowly and then steadily. We had not brought an umbrella, nor our raincoats, so she just held my hand tightly and we walked home in the rain, stopping occasionally to splash the mud puddles.

Grandfather Council and the Real Santa

My Grandfather Council was a unique man in many ways. He had very little formal education but was given a solid foundation in mathematics and literature by Mrs. Worth Pierce, a kind of foster mother and teacher who took him into her household when he was only about five years old to raise him as her own.

My grandfather was what he called a "semi-orphan." His father had been killed in a logging accident when he was just four. His mother knew she would be unable to provide proper care for him and his four sisters, so she arranged with Mr. and Mrs. Worth Pierce—of Pierce and Company—to help her raise her children. Granddaddy worked in the store as a boy, where he learned accounting and business practices from a young age. My great grandmother stayed in touch with him until her death in 1957.

Later, Granddaddy decided he wanted to be a lawyer, at a time when you didn't need a degree or to attend law school. He "read for the law," apprenticing under an attorney in Whiteville before eventually passing the bar exam. He never practiced law, however, because the Great North Carolina Lumber Company came to the area in the early part of the twentieth century and, shortly thereafter, hired my grandfather to run the company commissary. There were several large, semi-permanent logging camps down in the swamp. The camps included a commissary as well as housing, both collective and private, for the loggers and their families. And since he was also a lawyer, Granddaddy was appointed a magistrate and was in charge of maintaining law and order in the logging camp as well.

Magistrates had broad powers at that time. My grandfather would arrest unruly loggers on a Saturday night, lock them in the back of the commissary until Sunday morning, then load them all on a tram and take them to church at Bogue Chapel in Hallsboro where they had their own special section to sit in. After service he'd haul them back so they could get ready to go back to work on Monday morning. A unique arrangement, for certain, but it met the needs of the lumber company—and the law.

In 1945, just after World War II had ended, Grandfather Council opened his general store, Council and Company, right there in Hallsboro. He was fifty-five years old the day the store opened its doors. They sold just about anything the farmers and loggers in the community needed: clothes, food, farm supplies, appliances, and, later, heating oil for homes as well as tobacco curing oil.

My grandfather was a very religious man and a deacon in the Baptist church. He believed in a charitable and vengeful God, and he thought it important to practice what he preached in his Sunday school classes, including helping others whenever possible.

I remember one particular Christmas at the store from when I was just a little boy. It didn't look much like Christmas. The smoke from the lumber mills had mixed with the fog and intermittent light rain cast a gray cover over the little town of Hallsboro. It was 1956, and all the mills were booming business, and the little stores, including Council and Company, were decorated with colored lights around the doors and small show windows. Somebody had spelled out "Merry Christmas" in white glitter paint on one of the windows of the little soda shop next door.

But inside our store was an even more festive atmosphere. We had cut a pine tree from the woods right behind the store and placed it off to one side next to the appliances. My sister, my mother, and my Aunt Lucille let me help decorate it. Like our own tree at home, it wasn't a classic Christmas fir tree; it was a pine tree with significant gaps between the limbs, and it leaned a little no matter which way you turned it. But it was pretty, with big colored lights that blinked; a long string of stale popcorn wrapped around from the bottom to the top with tinsel icicles randomly placed all over; solid glass balls of red and green hung tenuously from the spindly pine needles; and a gold star on the top. Mama and Aunt Lucille questioned its aesthetic appeal, but my sister Linda and I thought it looked great.

We sold "record players" in the store—not stereos or sound systems but record players that played 33 ⅓, long-playing, "high fidelity" records as well as the smaller 45 RPM singles. That day we had put on a recording of Christmas music—Bing Crosby singing "White Christmas" was one of Mama's favorites—and turned up the sound loud enough to be heard all over the store.

Toys were displayed on shelves and tables along the side of the store. Cap guns and air rifles sat beside basketballs and footballs, assorted dolls, checkerboard and Monopoly games—and shiny new bikes with whitewall tires sat parked in neat rows along the store's floor. But it was the grocery side of the store that really told you it was the Christmas season. The produce section was filled with oranges, apples, grapes, bananas, and dried dates ... collards, sweet potatoes, Irish potatoes, cabbages, celery, and more. And right at the end of the produce counter was a special section of Christmas candy: "hard candy" with "hot" cinnamon and peppermint flavors, sticks of liquorice, orange slices, and my daddy's favorite: chocolate covered cherries. All those smells from the fruits and candy mingled with the music, the Christmas tree lights, and the toy display to create a magical feel that couldn't be duplicated, even in a grand store like Macy's in New York City.

It was into this wonderful, captivating atmosphere that Clarence Henderson arrived. Grandfather Council knew Clarence from his time working the commissary at the lumber mill, and by now our family knew him as well. Granddaddy had seen Clarence many times on the mill site, where he worked as an oiler—the man who kept the saws, conveyor belts, and everything else that turned turning.

It was almost closing time when Clarence came in, his face and his gait weary. I could smell the oil on him as soon as he came in the door. It was such a heavy smell, I could almost see it rise around him through the flakes of sawdust that covered his bibbed overalls and flannel shirt. A tiny stream of rain water ran down a crease in his wide-brimmed hat that had long ago lost its shape, and his high-toped brogan shoes daubed mud on the floor with every step he took. Clarence was a big man, over six-feet tall and two hundred pounds, and he wore the usual logger's uniform of denim overalls and a flannel shirt. His large, rough presence struck a sharp contract to Granddaddy Council, who was only about five-two and dressed, as always, in a white dress shirt and tie.

"Evening, Clarence. What can I do for you?" asked my grandfather.

"Well, I don't rightly know, Cap'n," he responded. (Cap'n was a title that denoted no rank but was a common name for any man who had supervised laborers at the mill.) "I gotta git some Christmas for my brother Chance's family. You know he got busted up pretty bad when that log chain broke the other day down in the swamp. That thing flew back and wrapped 'round his legs, you know. Broke both of 'em. He's stove up bad. Ain't worked in a couple o'weeks so he ain't got nothing for them kids for Christmas."

My grandfather did know the circumstances of the Henderson family and was a sympathetic and generous man, so his immediate response was, "Tell you what I'll do, Clarence. You go ahead and pick out what you think'll make a good Christmas, and we'll just make it a gift to you to help out."

Clarence didn't respond immediately. He just stood there and looked down at the floor as the Christmas music from the record player provided accompaniment for his thoughts. Finally, he said, "Cain't do that, Cap'n. You see, if you give the stuff to me it'll be your present, not mine. Them children is family. I got to do this myself."

Then he reached into the pocket of his old denim overalls and pulled out a hand full of change. "This is what I got. You know I cain't cipher. You count it out and tell me what can I get for it," Clarence instructed.

My grandfather took the change, counted it and said, "There's a dollar and twenty-one cents here. That'll buy a pretty good Christmas."

So, Clarence began to gather items in his arms. There was no shopping cart, no basket, just his big arms. He gathered some oranges and apples and then stopped at the candy counter as he looked at what he had gathered and then at my grandfather. "'Nough left for some candy?" he asked.

"Oh, yes. You got a lot left," was the response.

So, Clarence picked out a few pieces of hard candy and a couple of orange slices and then brought his armload to the cash register and placed it on the counter. As he looked over at the toy display, he asked "You reckon there's enough left to get the two little ones a toy apiece?"

"Oh, I think so," was the almost whispered response.

Clarence picked out a yo-yo for the boy and a Raggedy Ann doll for the girl and brought them to the counter. "What does all that come to, Cap'n?"

My grandfather pushed some buttons on an adding machine and said, "That comes to exactly a dollar and twenty cents." Then he reached in his pocket and took out a penny. "And here's your change."

Grandfather Council placed all of the items in a paper bag. As Clarence lifted the bag and stepped toward the door, he said, "Thank you, Cap'n. Y'all have a nice Christmas now."

I watched Clarence get in his car and drive away from the store. The sputter of the engine and the rattle of the old car seemed to fit in with the fog and the rain. But, then again, it could have been sleigh bells I heard instead.

Who Are Your People?

For almost three-quarters of a century, I have been a traveler. Sometimes I went to very faraway places like Europe. I have been to every state in the United States—except Hawaii and Alaska. I have visited all one hundred counties in North Carolina. In all those travels, someone always asked me, "Where are you from?" That usually happened shortly after they heard my Southern accent. My response often depended on where exactly I was and how broadly I had to begin identifying home.

Sometimes the question would be a little different. "Where are you from?" or "Where do you live?" were commonly heard the further out I ventured. As I got closer to home, "Where do you stay?" would be inevitably followed by, "Now, who are your people?"

In very faraway places, after establishing my American citizenship, I would further narrow my answer down to where I'm *from*. It always involved more than a place on a map.

Where I'm from is the American South. The weather is hot here. Humid hot. We drink a lot of sweet tea and soft drinks and lemonade, and sometimes a little bourbon with a little water. When the temperature gets below fifty degrees, we put on a jacket or sweater.

Where I'm from, two fellas named Martin Luther King Jr. and James Earl Ray were born. You might have heard of them. They both grew up in the same humid heat, but they handled it differently. One dreamed dreams and the other was a nightmare.

Where I'm from, Spanish moss hangs from cypress trees and bare pecan trees form filigree silhouettes in the winter sky.

Where I'm from, "Make yourself at home" is a command not a request.

Where I'm from, you can encounter rain and sunshine or motionless heat and cold wind can occur on the same day. And snow cones have nothing to do with the weather.

Where I'm from, we like the old roads, particularly the dirt ones. They not only get us from one place to the other, they transport us to and through our rural heritage that got paved over by the interstates.

Where I'm from, mosquitoes and "no-see-ums" provide the summer accompaniment to outdoor conversations, picnics, and concerts, and are the greatest deterrent to outdoor sex since her daddy's flashlight.

Where I'm from, tradition is a big deal. There are ways to do things—rituals—for everything from weddings to funerals to baptisms, hospital visits, how to greet people (shake hands, hugs, kisses, etc.), what and when and how to eat. Food is a part of almost every tradition and will, at some time, involve a casserole dish.

Where I'm from, almost every woman is, has been, or will be in some kind of beauty pageant. And believe me, they are proud of it. They rightfully believe that strong women are beautiful in their own way. My Granddaddy Council was not known to express his opinion about female beauty. But he did tell me, when I was a little boy, that if I was to become a Southern Gentleman, I should remember that "All women are beautiful; some are just more beautiful than others." I remember that.

C~

Where I live is a little more definitive.

Where I live, we say, "Yes, ma'am" and "No, ma'am," regardless of the woman's age.

Where I live, we have real, functional porches on our houses. They have real rocking chairs, usually a swing, and probably a small wicker table. People actually sit on the porches, either watching the traffic or talking to visitors. Discussion of politics is limited to local elections and gossip is encouraged.

Where I live, there are a lot of backyard parties. They are not called "barbecues." They are usually held in the late afternoon as the weather cools a little. They are lighted by paper lanterns, accompanied by beach music, and little ham sandwiches are served with a lime-green punch. Guests usually switch from crystal cups to little red solo cups as the evening wears on. The content of the cup usually changes as well.

Where I live, hurricanes blow tops off houses and flood kitchens on Tuesday and then generate prayers and food and neighborhood carpenters on Friday.

Where I live, mill whistles and church bells often ring at the same time. Sometimes for the same reason. The mills close from ten o'clock on Sunday morning until noon.

Where I live, Duke and Carolina fans only speak to each other at funerals and baptisms.

I narrow my answer down a little further in response to: "Where do you stay?"

Where I stay, a letter may be addressed to "Mr. and Mrs. Ray Wyche, 508 Hillsboro Rd., Hallsboro, NC," but it will be delivered to Mr. Ray and Miss Melba at the green and white house across from the Baptist church.

Where I stay, we wave at people we don't even know, assuming we probably do know them, but they might be driving a different car.

Where I stay, tobacco gum never comes in a package, but it has been known to add a distinctive flavor to a watermelon "busted" in the heat of a tobacco field.

Where I stay, just down the road from me are gray, weathered cabins and white-columned mansions, chapels, and cathedrals. The same store where I buy my khaki pants sells debutante gowns and Daisy Duke shorts; pickup trucks are driven by men in tuxedos to the country club; and pretty girls in jeans and T-shirts arrive by limousine at the Country Music Shack down by the river.

When growing up (where I stay), dinner (what some refer to as "lunch") would be eaten at the house of whomever we happened to be playing with.

Where I stay, we had Sunday dinner at Grandma's. Mama fried the chicken, sister brought the snap beans, Aunt Lou the potato salad. And Grandma provided the fried corn bread (no sugar), and Granddaddy asked the Lord to bless it all.

⟋

And who are my people?

All my people wear shoes ... most of the time.

Most of my people have dual names: Billy Joe, Ann Marie, etc. However, if Mama ever calls you by all three names (William Henry Thompson!), that is not a good sign.

My people sing and play music. They sing in church choirs and oratorio groups and swing bands and country bands and rock bands and school bands. They sing the blues and they sing praise songs. And sometimes they just sing to themselves because that's their most appreciative audience.

My people are proud of who we are, even those we know who are scoundrels. We acknowledge our faults and exalt our virtues and vow, with the Lord's help, to do better next time. We can't say what other people think doesn't matter to us, but we believe that what we think of *each other* matters more.

All my people aren't bound together by birth. Some are bound together by cultural heritage that goes beyond color or race or creed.

We each perceive that culture differently. Sometimes we wish we could change some of the past, the parts we don't like. But as Mr. Faulkner said, "In the South, the past isn't dead; it's not even past." I've found that we are all more alike than we are different; we share the same hopes and dreams. Each of us has the same heritage, a shared past that can't be changed. For some folks, that heritage may not be so good. But it is our heritage, a shared heritage, whether we think it's good or bad.

Part 2
THE COOL BREEZE OF FRIENDSHIP

The Cool Breeze of Friendship

I've got two pairs of white buck shoes in my closet. One pair is about worn out, so I bought the second pair to wear so I wouldn't look as used up as that old buckskin. That's what happens sometimes, you know. Our countenance reflects the condition of our shoes. That's where the old expression "down at the heels" comes from. I still wear the old shoes when I want to be comfortable and don't have to worry about looking proper.

White buckskin shoes are proper footwear when you want to feel stylish during the summer, particularly down here in the South. They go with just about everything, especially a seersucker suit of any color. I've got blue, gray, and brown seersucker suits I love to wear. I saw a light red (okay, pink) seersucker suit one time that I thought about buying, but I decided it made me look too much like an ice cream salesman.

Now, white bucks are stylish for *summer* wear, because you just don't wear white shoes before Easter or after Labor Day. Some other rules that have developed over the years are: wear white socks with white bucks, do not wear them with black slacks, and keep them only moderately clean so they don't look like they are brand new. White bucks and khakis are always correct. (Down here in the South, khakis are proper attire for just about every occasion, short of a formal wedding or a funeral.) White bucks are dress shoes, but unlike other dress shoes, you can't polish them. You just use a stiff brush or a big rubber eraser to get the scuff marks off. With other dress shoes, you can polish them to such a high sheen, you can almost see your reflection. My old bucks don't shine, but they reflect a lot.

When I look at those old shoes, I remember wearing some just like them to lawn parties (called "garden parties" if there was a lot of shrubbery around) back in my youth, where there were beautiful girls in bright sun dresses that showed off their dutifully acquired tans. There was usually a band set up on the patio. Beach music wafted through the night air, mixing with the smell of perfume and freshly-cut grass. Paper lanterns suspended in the trees would cast a soft glow like stardust over us while my white bucks shuffled and spun and flirted with the dyed-to-match pumps of the girl whose fingertips just touched mine as we danced the night away.

Later, another pair of bucks, just like those before, would transport me to hundreds of festivals, celebrating everything imaginable in small towns and big cities throughout the South—events that brought together the diversity of the community while extolling the unique element that justified each celebration. My white bucks fit right in with the boots and flip-flops, high-heels and sandals. There was always a luncheon or a pig pickin' where everybody wore little name tags and greeted each other with hugs. Sometimes we'd sit at picnic tables or on bales of straw, otherwise we'd find any flat surface where we could place our paper plates and plastic cups while we stood and talked and laughed. And there would always be a bluegrass band playing under a pecan tree, its high-pitched harmonies and fast-paced instruments setting a tone of excitement and optimism.

I've worn my white bucks to many, many wedding ceremonies and receptions. I've worn them to outdoor nuptials where threatening clouds in the distance were dismissed as being too ephemeral to cast a cloud on the occasion. But I have also run for shelter as those clouds dampened the proceedings, everybody waiting too late to escape getting wet. On these occasions, my white bucks would get wet and muddy as I dashed across a drenched lawn, or raced to my car through a dirt parking lot. But those shoes clean up pretty well, surviving with a touch of class.

I had a friend who lived at Wrightsville Beach back during the early '80s. His house had a big, wrap-around porch always full of cut flowers and ferns. White wicker furniture was spread around the porch; the blue and white print cushions lent light and color to the comfortable resting spot. Everything was very ordered but relaxed. After a garden party at Airlie during the Azalea Festival one year, he had a few friends over, and I noticed how all the men, including me, wore white bucks. The shoes just sorta came together with the porch ... and the gin and tonics and the little finger sandwiches ... and the boiled peanuts.

When we get right down to the reality of style, white bucks are just shoes. They are attire for the feet, support for the body, and an accompaniment to the clothes we wear. But it seems to me that my particular white bucks have a unique quality. They create memories.

One Giant Moment in Time: Rube and Hester McCray

Few moments in history can compare to Lewis and Clark setting out from St. Louis to explore the newly-acquired Louisiana Purchase; Christopher Columbus pointing his ships west to a new world; or Buzz Aldrin and Neil Armstrong blasting off from Cape Canaveral toward the moon. But in my personal history, such a time was in December 1965. I don't think those explorers felt any more trepidation than I did when I stood at the door of Flemington Hall on the campus of what was then Boys Home of Lake Waccamaw. That day changed my personal history as much as the ventures of those explorers changed the history of the world.

I had come home to Hallsboro for Christmas. I was just twenty-two years old at the time; Claudia and I had been married only four months, and we had been teaching at Stedman High School in Cumberland County, North Carolina. I don't know why Mrs. Hester McCray had not called me in Stedman, but she left a message with Mama to have me call her when we got to Hallsboro.

I'd met Mrs. McCray through our mutual involvement with the community chorus; she had been the director of the community choir while I was in high school and college. That was a tenuous connection at most, however, since I had been just one of many in that group.

So, when Mama gave me the message, I was curious as to what Mrs. McCray could possibly want with me. When I called her, she asked if I could come down to the lake and meet with her and Mr. McCray. I agreed, still not knowing what she wanted.

The McCrays lived in a big, white house called Flemington Hall, which was situated on a hill overlooking Lake Waccamaw. It was an imposing building that also served as the administration building for Boys Home, a home for boys who had lost or been removed from their families for various unfortunate reasons. The McCrays lived on the second floor and operated the home.

The home had been built by a lumberman who personally selected the wood for the construction of the large, two-story house with a porch on the second level that looked out over the lake. It was a little intimidating for a young man from Hallsboro; the home was only about four miles from town but a million miles from the kind of home I was used to.

Mrs. McCray met me at the door and I followed her into a large living room. To one side of the room was a staircase that led to a landing and a small porch, then on to the upstairs living quarters. It was a Southern home with a lot of open space, windows, and doors that allowed the breeze from the lake to alleviate heat during the summer months.

But the centerpiece of the living room was a black grand piano situated beside the stairs. Mrs. McCray was an accomplished pianist. She always played piano while I was in her community choir, so I was not surprised she would have a piano in her home. But I had rarely seen a grand piano in a private residence.

As we sat in the living room, Mrs. McCray was the perfect lady but very businesslike. She hadn't called me there for tea; she wanted me to come and work with her. "With her" was an important part of the conversation. She had organized a group of the boys to perform for various functions on behalf of the home. In fact, the group was becoming a big part of the public relations program, as well as a great educational opportunity for those boys in the choir. She wanted me to help build the group into a more formal choir and to expand their role in the promotion of the home. She would continue to be the accompanist, and we would work together in selecting the music and teaching the boys who would be selected by audition only. The entire home housed 100 boys, divided between six different residencies on campus. About twenty were selected for the choir.

At some point during our meeting, Mrs. McCray said she wanted me to meet and talk with her husband, Rube, about the job. As if on cue, Mr. McCray came down the stairs and joined us.

R.N. "Rube" McCray was a big man. He was about six-and-a-half feet tall and weighed about 280 pounds. He didn't so much walk down those stairs as descend them, like Moses coming down from the mountain. He was the most imposing figure I had (or still have) ever seen. He had thinning blond hair swept back on a big head, a smile to match his stature, and his bare hand was about the size of a baseball glove. When he reached out to greet me, my relatively small hand disappeared in his firm grasp. I was in awe.

When he said, "Sit down here on the couch, William, and let's talk about this choir thing," it wasn't so much an invitation as it was a command. So, I joined him on that big couch, he at one end and me at the other, while Mrs. McCray sat in a chair across the room. She had turned me over to him.

During the next hour or so, I became less intimidated and more comfortable with this man. He wanted to know about me, my family, my education, and what I liked and didn't like about everything from books and music to horses and sports. He seemed genuinely interested in me. I would learn over the years how Rube McCray had the ability to make everyone he met feel important, at ease, like the way I felt that afternoon. That's why he was so well-suited to head Boys Home: he cared about every one of the residents who came there—and they knew it.

Mr. McCray was a smart businessman who understood the importance of public relations, particularly as part of broad efforts to raise funds for charitable organizations like Boys Home. The Boys Home Choir became a crucial element in that effort.

While Mrs. McCray and I worked with the boys to produce a quality of musical performance we could be proud of, one that would show supporters what music could do for youngsters from unfortunate situations, Mr. McCray sought out ways to get us before the public.

Mr. McCray knew how to get the most from every investment. During our initial discussion that December afternoon, he outlined what my duties would be. There was a relatively small staff at that time, so everyone had multiple duties. In addition to the choir, I was to help establish an on-campus elementary school and act as liaison with the local high school many of the boys attended. I would also be a counselor for two cottages of boys (sixteen boys in each of six cottages), write a monthly newsletter to be mailed to contributors and fundraising letters to prospective donors, and speak to civic clubs around the state. In exchange, I was given a nice little house to live in and $6,000 a year (a lot more than I had been making as a school teacher).

Rube McCray had taken an unusual route to Boys Home. He was an athlete who grew up in the mountains of Tennessee and used his considerable athletic ability to attend college on basketball and football scholarships. Eventually, he became a coach. He wasn't just any coach. He was able to build quality athletic programs that had never been seen at the institutions he served. As football coach and athletic director at the College of William and Mary, he drew national attention as he took the post-World War II teams to championships against UNC at Chapel Hill, Duke, Alabama, and other bigger schools around the country.

Unfortunately, that attention raised questions about the standards for qualifying some of the players. The program was accused of allowing students who had not met academic requirements to play. Many of the team's players were former soldiers whose military service had put them in excellent physical condition, but they struggled with academics. While this is a more widely-known practice now, it was a big scandal back in

1951. Mr. McCray never admitted direct involvement, but he accepted the responsibility. He resigned from his job at William and Mary and then opened an automobile dealership in West Point, Virginia.

But selling cars was not meant for a man like Rube McCray. When Boys Home at Lake Waccamaw began looking for a director to succeed founder A.D. Peacock, a friend of Mr. McCray told them he knew just the man.

Mr. McCray took the experience he had gained in working with boys on athletic teams to working with boys who needed to overcome the circumstances that had taken them out of their homes and to the campus at Lake Waccamaw.

In those early days, the admissions process was relatively simple: if a community member knew of a boy who needed help, they told the local social service organization and then that boy often came to Boys Home. Mr. McCray knew each boy, where he came from, and why he was there. Most importantly, every boy knew him.

If there were problems at school, in the cottage, or on the athletic field, there were counselors like me to talk with the boys. But it almost always came down to a talk with Mr. McCray to get it worked out. One of the most memorable and frequent sights was Mr. McCray walking across the campus, that big hand and arm around a boy's shoulder, talking out a problem. He didn't believe that having a boy come into his office and sit in a chair opposite his desk was an effective way to solve problems. He believed in what he called "Reality Therapy," interaction with the boys in everyday situations. When boys were assigned chores on the campus, there was usually a counselor—and Mr. McCray—right there with them, whether it was mowing the lawns, harvesting the pecan crop, or cleaning stalls on the farm. Admittedly, that was a simpler time with simpler solutions. But it worked.

Mr. McCray also brought a unique approach to gaining support for Boys Home. At that time in America, civic clubs flourished in every city and hamlet. There was at least one civic service organization, even in the most rural towns. Mr. McCray once told me one reason civic clubs were so numerous and active was because they were made up of so many veterans who had served in World War II and Korea. At war, they had accomplished so much as a part of a group with a collective effort. So, it stood to reason they could use that same collective spirit of service to preserve what they had fought for. So, those veterans became Civitans and Lions and Jaycees and Kiwanians and Rotarians and Optimists.

Mr. McCray realized the tremendous potential for getting these organizations to support Boys Home. After all, the home's founding board of trustees was composed of Civitans and Lions in nearby Whiteville. In bringing all those clubs together with one continuous statewide effort, he accomplished something that had never existed before—nor has it since: the continuous support of several different independent organizations for a single project.

One of my titles was "Civic Club Coordinator," certainly the only one in the country. That meant I talked to a lot of local clubs as well as district and state conventions. My first major speaking engagement was to make a report to the North Carolina Lions State Convention in Raleigh. I was a little like Barney Fife in a shootout at high noon; I was so nervous about speaking to such a large group in Raleigh Memorial Auditorium. This was the first time I'd spoken to a group of that size without the support of a choir behind me. I don't know how many people were actually there, but I'm sure it was more than the combined population of Hallsboro and Lake Waccamaw.

I wanted to do my best, so I typed out all the information and began to memorize every word of it. I asked if I could do a "practice run" for Mr. and Mrs. McCray, and they agreed. I met them in their living room that night to rehearse. After a glance at my paper, I began to recite my speech. I had only gone a minute or so when Mr. McCray stopped me. He said, "That won't work. You'll be nervous and forget the words you wrote.

Don't try to memorize everything. Just tell 'em what you know. Tell 'em about the boys."

I made my report to the Lions convention. It went well and, of course, Mr. McCray knew how it had gone before I got back home. On the following Monday morning, he told me he had some other groups he wanted me to speak to. So, I began a unique journey across North Carolina that would take me the length and breadth of the state. I would get to know not only all the roads (even before the first interstate) but also a lot of great people in the big cities and little communities. I became of part of organizations that not only supported Boys Home but hundreds of other charities as well. As I got to know the club members from different organizations, they would ask me to emcee various activities they sponsored. These activities were not necessarily connected to Boys Home but included festival celebrations (for spot fish, dogwoods, collards, cotton, tobacco, etc.), beauty pageants, races, talent shows, and luncheons. I was a part of every imaginable festival and community celebration, and was afforded a once-in-a-lifetime opportunity to know my state, the geography, and the culture. And, I was cheap—usually free—since my involvement created good will for Boys Home. As an added benefit, the organizations got both a speaker and a singer. Later, I would use that experience in my newspaper and magazine columns, then in my books. I don't know how many speeches I've made since then, or how many people I've talked to, but I still approach every occasion in the same way. I just tell 'em what I know.

⁓

There's an old cliché that says, "Behind every successful man is a woman pushing him on." I think to some extent that may have been the case with Mrs. Hester McCray. She was certainly with Rube all the way, through the ups and downs and triumphs and tragedies of his career. She was a big part of Boys Home, though she was never a paid employee. (After Mr. McCray's death she served as Interim Director until a successor could be found.) It didn't take me long to learn the Boys Home Choir was Mrs. McCray's idea. And that was just one of her ideas. She also promoted the idea that a beautiful campus was a part of the program of care; she knew the attractiveness would help heal emotional wounds and build up flagging spirits. So, she oversaw the planting of flowers and shrubs to beautify the campus. I often saw her out on the campus, planting flowers or pulling weeds. It was probably indicative of her Southern upbringing that she always wore a dress, no long pants or shorts, when working with her plants. Pants would have been improper. I think her actual word was "tacky."

Once we got the choir rehearsed and ready to the point we thought we could do so, the McCrays and I put together a tour of civic clubs. We didn't know it yet, but the tour was kind of a rehearsal for what was to become a tradition: the Christmas Show.

In those days before video tape, we would travel to every television station in North Carolina, as well as some in Virginia and South Carolina, between Thanksgiving and Christmas, performing on local shows. We would leave early and travel in three station wagons. Mr. McCray would drive the front car, followed by the car driven by one of the older boys and then I would drive the third car.

Almost always, Mrs. McCray would ride with me. We would talk about the music program and often she would review a newsletter or appeal letter I had written. Before coming to Lake Waccamaw, she had been an English teacher. I once said that after Mrs. McCray reviewed my writing, the document would die. All the red-penciled corrections indicated it had surely bled to death. But I learned a lot about writing.

Beyond working with the choir, Mrs. McCray worked with me on my own music as well. She wanted me to perform as often as possible. "That's how you grow," she told me. So, she would find a piece of music she thought I should learn and we would practice in the home's living room, at that big black grand piano. She would have me sing for the wives of members of the board of trustees during board meetings, or for what she called, (soirees), irregularly scheduled gatherings of ladies in the area who alternated visiting in homes for a musical presentation or a reading by a poet or writer.

My most memorable soirée was held at a home on the lake. Mrs. McCray liked Broadway music, particularly anything by Rogers and Hammerstein. On that occasion she chose "The Soliloquy" from *Carrousel* for me to sing. For those unfamiliar with the song, it is sung by the central character, Billy Bigelow, a roguish young man who marries and finds that he is soon to become a father. (Coincidentally, my daughter, Mari, had just been born.) The realization of imminent fatherhood and the awareness of his poor financial situation brings on Billy's commitment to do better. It is a very moving piece and I sang it with the appropriate emotion. In fact, Mrs. McCray and I were both in tears at the end as I sang, "I'll go out and make it . . . or steal it . . . or take it . . . or die!" Mrs. McCray and I both were in tears. To break the mood, Mrs. McCray said, "I bet if you sang that for Rube, he'd give you a raise."

Mrs. McCray took the same personal interest in the boys as she did in me. If she ever learned that one of the boys had a serious girlfriend, Mrs. McCray would have the couple up for dinner in the private quarters of Flemington Hall. It was an opportunity for etiquette lessons and, in her motherly mode, to find out more about the girl.

When people first met Mr. and Mrs. McCray (I never was presumptuous enough to call them Hester and Rube), the couple may have seemed to have contrasting personalities. Mr. McCray was a big, outgoing, hail-fellow-well-met kind of gentleman who drew people to him. He had an undefinable charisma that made him the center of attention wherever he went. But behind that good ol' country boy image was an unmatched intellectual who understood people better than anybody I'd ever met.

Mrs. McCray was the epitome of the refined Southern lady. She had an appreciation for the arts, was a very talented painter, and enjoyed all kinds of crafts. But she also had the ability to make people feel at ease, even in formal situations. She appreciated the finer things in life, but she valued honesty and genuine effort above all else. She had a work ethic that challenged those who worked with her. On one of those choir trips, as she sat in the car with me, we talked about the possibility of her retirement. She mentioned she had no plans to ever retire, saying, "I'd rather wear out than rust out."

I never heard either of the McCrays complain about their past misfortunes. They were always optimistic about tomorrow. Maybe it was their heritage; maybe their faith. They were both very aware of life's hills and valleys, but they knew the key to success and happiness was to stay focused on the mountaintop. They tried to pass that attitude along to me and the hundreds of boys who came to Lake Waccamaw.

One of those boys was Gary Faircloth. Gary's brother, Ronald, had preceded Gary to the Lake Waccamaw campus. Their family had been disrupted when their father left and their mother was unable to care for them. The boys had been left to fend for themselves on the streets of Fayetteville and the bank of the Cape Fear River that ran not too far from their house. Though Gary was too young to come to Boys Home when Ron did, both eventually adapted well to life at the home, having been in the custody of social services previously. Ron was a good athlete, and with Mr. McCray's help, got a scholarship to play football at the University of North Carolina at Chapel Hill. He graduated from that institution, came back to work for Boys Home for a while, then went into the insurance business and later developed a chain of formal-wear shops, among other enterprises, before getting married and raising a family.

Gary took a different road to success. After high school graduation, he got a job at the local paper mill but decided he wanted more. He went back to school, and earned a degree in social work and juvenile correction from East Carolina University. After a stint as a juvenile probation officer, he also came back to work at Boys Home. Gary worked at the expanded campus in Huntersville, north of Charlotte, and when that campus transitioned to a girls' campus, he came to the lake. He was married with children when he worked at the Huntersville campus, and lived on campus at both places. He became more involved in the financial development of the program and eventually became the Director of Development. And when the opportunity came for him to move to a higher position at a larger institution in Michigan, Gary made the move to Starr Commonwealth and was in charge of their financial development.

$\sim$

After I had worked with Boys and Girls Homes of North Carolina (off and on) for nearly thirty-five years, I was selected by the board of trustees to succeed General Stuart Sherman as President in 2001. When I decided to retire in 2008, Gary was the first person I called, even before I'd told the board of trustees of my plans. I wanted to know if he would be interested in "coming back home." I couldn't think of anybody who would have been more qualified to lead Boys and Girls Homes into a future full of changes. Gary had every experience: from resident, to counselor, financial development officer (including the unique involvement with civic clubs), and administrative ability. And beyond that, Gary was "one of my boys." He was a senior when I came to the campus in 1966, and was a member of my first choir. Over the years we became good friends. I tutored Gary in some of his college classes, sang for his wedding, and worked with him in the financial development office. We formed a bond like brothers.

So, when Gary assumed the role of President at Boys and Girls Homes, it was a little like completing the circle. He maintained the organization's tradition of caring as it assumed its place in the modern world of child care. And at the base of all of Gary's qualifications was the role model we shared in common: Rube McCray.

David Ariail: The Johnny Appleseed of Community Theater

To use the parlance of the time when we first met, David Ariail was a "cool dude." It was 1979 and I had just been hired as general manager for the outdoor drama *Strike at the Wind* in Pembroke, North Carolina. I hired David as the director of the historic play as we began its fourth season, though it was the first year for both of us. At first glance, we couldn't have been more unalike. David was tall and lanky with a nonchalant air of confidence that made people automatically feel comfortable around him. He had a beard and shaggy hair, much in contrast to my own clean-cut "business image." I assumed it was just a part of his "theater persona." But he was not the flamboyant dramatist at all. He was low-key; nothing seemed to rattle him as he took every challenge in stride, seldom raising his low, vibrant voice even when giving direction to actors on the open outdoor stage. While I wore a coat and tie every day and remained scheduled down to every minute, David was the artist. He laughed easily. And though I shared his appreciation for the art, I was the businessman.

In retrospect, it's easy to see why he was so capable and confident. David had a background in community theater that bode him well in working with those folks just getting a taste of theater, as well as professionals with a great deal of experience. Flexibility is a real asset in almost every creative endeavor. When you combine that flexibility with a broad range of talents and the ability to be unphased by unexpected circumstances, you have someone well-suited to deal with the creative, quirky world of theater.

At the dress rehearsal just before opening night of *Strike at the Wind*, a lighting technician took offense at how he was listed in the show program. In the midst of a tantrum, he told David he was leaving the show. In the process of leaving, while still storming about the stage, the technician began disassembling and tearing out all the lighting for the show, including the control panel. Gels were strewn all over the stage, wires disconnected, tall lighting trees pushed to the ground. It was a mess. And the show was to open in less than twenty-four hours.

Without getting the least upset, David gathered the remaining technical crew as well as some of the actors and began to reassemble and focus the lighting. Remember, outdoor dramas take place at night; the incident with the technician took place just prior to dawn. It is extremely difficult to light an outdoor set in the daylight. But because David was so knowledgeable about every aspect of theater production and because he had melded together such a great team, he was able to bring everything back to where it was supposed to be in time for the show to open on time and to rave reviews.

Theater drama is not limited to performances on the stage.

David's flexibility, creativity, and personality are just some of the reasons he has been so successful in establishing and maintaining community theaters across the state. When he graduated from the University of North Carolina at Chapel Hill in the late '70s, he had a bachelor's degree in English and a master's degree in theater. Like so many other graduates in that field, he thought New York was the place to be. But a call from the North Carolina Arts Council convinced him to become an artist-in-residence, and he did so for several small communities across the state.

From there, David moved into establishing community theaters. He became a playwright-in-residence in the Anson County community of Wadesboro. That led to a request from the town council to build a theater; so David took charge of the project to renovate the public library's basement, build a stage, and recruit actors, carpenters, electricians, and others. The opening play was, appropriately, *Our Town* and played to sold-out audiences for eight nights—a long run for an upstart company in a town of about 5,000 people.

David continued to be the Johnny Appleseed of Community Theater as he moved on to similar success in Lenoir and Rockingham. When he got to Rockingham in Richmond County, he persuaded the owner of an old movie theater to donate the building to the town of Rockingham and asked the town to pay for the water, electricity, and insurance. The theater association agreed, began a fundraising program, and eventually opened a permanent theater: the Richmond County Community Theater. David stayed there for thirty years, and he directed over a hundred shows (five shows a year plus three children's shows) involving over a thousand people. He wrote many of the plays, continuing to feed the creative spirit that got him into theater in the first place.

David is an actor, playwright, director, and master of stagecraft, but not many people know that he never intended to get into theater. He left Fayetteville when he graduated from high school, went to Chapel Hill with no particular goal in mind, got on the basketball team as a walk-on, and in the course of his undergraduate work, got into theater and found out he liked writing plays. He had found his calling.

In addition to his work with the renowned Carolina Playmakers, one summer David joined the cast of *Unto These Hills*. He also wrote *The Inherited Freedom* for the Caldwell Bicentennial Commission. Those endeavors provided him with the unique experience that helped him be so successful during our time with *Strike at the Wind*.

Which brings us to David and me as we sat down recently to talk for the first time in over thirty years. It seemed like only yesterday we had worked together to put on that outdoor drama in Robeson County. The conversation was breezy, comfortable, as if we had just seen each other the day before. We reminisced about those "long-ago days" and caught up on what we had been doing in the interim.

When I asked David if he ever wished he had gone on to New York, he said, "No. It's important to remain where you can achieve something." He has achieved a lot, and has made a tremendous contribution to his community of Richmond County, as well as other towns where he planted the seed of community theater. He's made a difference in thousands of lives. The people of Richmond County thought enough of him to vote him the Chamber of Commerce Citizen of the Year in 1989.

David hadn't aged much visibly since I last saw him. He was still thin, though his hair was gray, and he still smiled as he talked. Like every actor, he talked with his body, moving his hands, sitting on the edge of the sofa, then spreading his long arms over the back of it. He still had the same melliferous voice.

I asked him why he thought he was so successful in getting small communities involved in theater. He said, "Don't play for the big time. Keep good people around you. People in small towns love the arts as much as the people in big cities. It's important to give them a chance to experience it, to be a part of it."

As we sat in the sunny dining area of David's beautiful home there in Rockingham, David suddenly said, "Look there! That's our resident white squirrel!" I turned to see a beautiful, completely white squirrel scramble across the back yard and then stop, standing erect near the back steps.

How appropriate, I thought. *Right here in his back yard. Something so unique, as unique as David himself.*

Bus Hubbard: Tree Surgeon

Sometime ago I was on the campus of the University of North Carolina at Chapel Hill. Although much of the campus seems to be in a perpetual modernizing state of construction, destruction, or reconstruction, most of the campus is a beautiful, tradition-laden setting that inspires the pursuit of education. There are some areas of arboreal serenity that perhaps encourage academic contemplation or, at the very least, provide a respite from the "paper chase." In some areas where students and faculty walk hurriedly from building to building, there are trees and shrubs that can provide some insufficient insulation from the non-academic world. It was in such a setting that I met William "Bus" Hubbard, a friend of a friend who I was told I just had to meet. Part woodsman and part artist, Bus is a man who creates beauty by cutting away what is ugly, a man who is a major element in creating and maintaining the green beauty of the campus.

Hurricane Hazel didn't exactly follow Bus to the university, but it came sweeping across the campus shortly after he got there in 1954. Just a few months prior to the storm and its subsequent major clean-up, the young man from Chatham County had been working for a construction company, building the new hospital in Chapel Hill. "I got tired of trying to push a loaded wheelbarrow up a board, and I heard about a job opening in the grounds department at the school. I got the job the same day I applied for it," he recalled during one of our visits.

Since that time, Bus Hubbard has become an institution within an institution. Since the 1950s, he has been the "Resident Tree Surgeon" on campus, a fount of knowledge regarding the care and feeding of trees and shrubs. But most importantly, Bus has gained the respect and admiration of the people he has worked with over the last half of a century. One fall afternoon several years ago as I talked to Bus about his long career, a particular phrase kept coming back over and over in our conversation: "I love my job."

"What has kept you here all these years?" I'd asked.

"I love my job. I like coming to work every morning. I like the people I work with. I like cuttin' trees. I get a lot of satisfaction out of what I do. I just enjoy it," he said.

Our conversation took place in one of the maintenance buildings. It was a cloudy day and the groundskeeping crew was about to stop for the day. Bus sat in an old metal chair, his body erect but comfortable. A naturally sturdy man, he had gained some weight over the years, but being so active kept him healthy regardless. That day, as on most days, he was smiling and affable, even at the end of a busy day. Although it was not a particularly cold day, he wore a denim jacket. There were flecks of sawdust on the jacket, residue from his labors. Bus trims trees, you know. And after over sixty years of trimming trees, he doesn't wear glasses.

We had one of the most enjoyable conversations I'd ever had. Bus was a lot like the folks I grew up with. He grew up on a tenant farm in Chatham County but soon realized farming was not something he wanted to do for the rest of his life. However, we talked about our shared love of the land as well as some of the travails that go with tending to it. We talked about cool, sweet-tasting well water. We talked about the feel of newly-plowed dirt on bare feet. We talked about hauling fertilizer in two-hundred-pound burlap bags, about cropping tobacco in the hot sun, and about how hard it was to make a living farming.

An old aphorism came to mind: "Farming is a great life if you've got another way to make a living." Realizing just that, Bus had come to Chapel Hill, first helping in the construction of the hospital, then working in the grounds department at the university ever since. He continued to live with his family for a while. "Back then, the school would let somebody drive one of the trucks home with 'em, and all of us that lived down that way would ride back and forth to work on that truck," he explained. Later, he moved to Durham where he and his wife now live. He provides his own transportation these days. "One reason they let us ride the truck was 'cause on twenty-five cents an hour we couldn't afford to get to work any other way," he laughed.

I thought that in the long passage of his years on campus, Bus would have developed some strong opinions on how the times have affected the university. What did he think about the controversy and demonstrations back in the days of "the Speaker Ban" of the early '60s? What did he think about the Tar Heel sports programs over the years? He didn't have much to say, if anything, about those and other similar topics. His interests were more mundane.

"I've climbed near 'bout every tree on this campus. I climbed the Davie Poplar many times. I've mowed the quad around the Old Well with a little hand-pushed mower. I've kept up the yards of every president since Dr. Friday. I liked 'em all and we got along fine." Bus has his own ideas about what's important at the university.

Bus is in good shape physically, particularly for a man seventy-six years old. I wondered how in all those years of climbing trees, he had avoided disabling injuries. I figured all that climbing and exercise helped.

He explained, "Well, exercise helps, but my first supervisor, Mr. Dunsmore, was a good teacher. He taught me how to climb and to rig my ropes so I wouldn't fall. He told me I had to trust myself and my ropes.

"When he started teaching me, he'd go up on the tree with me to help build my confidence. He'd pick a tree where nobody would see me if I made a mistake. Took the pressure off me. I learned by doing. I wasn't afraid after I learned to trust my ropes."

Bus still often uses the rope riggings today to prune the trees and "definitely don't use any spikes to climb a tree. Worse thing you can do," he added.

"We got more machinery now. When I first come we just used all hand tools. When we had to rake leaves, it was done by hand and we'd rake the leaves onto a sheet. Lifted it by hand and hauled it away by hand. It was hard work and you had to keep up. The older fellows would leave you behind if you didn't keep up," he said.

And when the storms came, it was still manual labor that cleaned up the wreckage. "When the trees got blowed down, I'd be the one to saw 'em up. We'd have a crew of usually three men. Sometimes we had to work 'round the clock, sleep in the shop a few hours, then get back at it. Everybody worked after a storm. When it snowed, we had to clear every walk before we could go home. There's a lot of walks on this campus!"

Listening to Bus reminisce about his years with the university made me wonder how he was able to maintain such a career. I asked him what advice he would give to a young man who wanted to follow in his footsteps. He came up with what I called "Bus's Rules for Getting Along."

1. "Never make a man mad. If the folks you work with get stirred up, leave 'em alone 'til things get right."
2. "Don't stop work to talk with the boss man when he comes around. If he asked you something, answer him. Otherwise keep on working."
3. "Know what you're doing and learn to do it the best you can."
4. "If you don't like what you're doing, go find something else 'cause you won't do a good job and that's not fair."
5. "Always respect the other man's job. Even if you can do it [his job], it's his job."

Bus Hubbard is a unique man in many ways. There aren't many men who can truthfully say they love their job. There aren't many men who are the best in their chosen craft. (Bus teaches aspiring tree surgeons from other universities the intricacies of his job.) There aren't many men who have gained the respect and admiration of their fellow workers for nearly fifty years. There aren't many men who possess the skill to transpose ordinary trees and shrubs into enduring beauty.

Whether he knows it or admits it, Bus has had a positive effect on many of the people he has worked with on the university campus. His supervisors, "the boss men," have only the highest praise for his ability and dedication to his job. His fellow workers admire him for his knowledge of his craft. In a business most often associated with toughness and where machismo flows like resin in a young pine, I detected just a bit of softness when Bus's name came up. "Six crews have all died on me," he said as he reflected wistfully on years of working together, mowing, trimming, raking, digging, and supporting nature in a world of academia. Bus, the natural world, and the people around him are all mutually supportive.

What does such a dedicated man like Bus do in his free time? He maintains the lawns of families in the area. Many afternoons after work and on weekends, he'll leave the campus to rake, mow lawns, and trim shrubbery for families, many of whom he has helped for over thirty years. "I love my job," he said. "It's my hobby too."

On my last visit with Bus, I met him at the Friday Center, a relatively new part of the university campus. The parking lot is divided by rows of beautiful trees whose seasonal gold and green leaves contrast with the gray of the concrete around them. It was almost noon when I got there. Before heading to lunch, Bus and the crew cleaned up the tree debris.

As the other men loaded limbs that had been trimmed that morning, I saw Bus walk toward one of the small trees at the corner of the parking lot. He walked easily, comfortable with the small chain saw he carried. With one easy motion, he started the saw and immediately began to trim some of the lower limbs of the tree. In just a few minutes, he had completed his task.

I asked, "Bus, how did you know which limbs to cut off?"

"You gotta know what you want it to look like. Then you cut away everything else," he replied. There was no technical jargon, no long essay on what should or shouldn't be beautiful, just an artist's sense of what he needed to do. I had heard that sculptor's response before, a tongue-in-cheek response to a request for an artist's explanation of artistic discretion, but in Bus's answer, I thought there was real sincerity and knowledge.

As I look back on my visits with Bus, I remember Joyce Kilmer's poem, "Trees," that we all learned back in school. I can't remember the entire poem, but I do remember the last line, "But only God can make a tree." I certainly don't disagree with Mr. Kilmer in that regard. But I do think God might have an assistant named Bus Hubbard to help keep the trees beautiful on the Chapel Hill campus.

If there was ever a man who taught me to be happy and thankful for being able to work at a job I love, it was Bus.

Pap Bellamy

Pap Bellamy was the first black man I ever really knew. He worked for my family at our store there in Hallsboro. He was working there when I was born during the middle of World War II, and he was still employed there when he died in 1976. I don't know when he was born and neither did he. Not many black folks back then had birth certificates. In any case, Pap had always seemed old to me.

His real name was Oscar, but my grandfather, Dave Council, the head of the family business, was the only person I ever heard call him that. My Aunt Lucille was the company bookkeeper and wrote "Oscar" in the payroll charts, but she paid cash money to "Pap" every week.

Pap was a small man in stature, maybe about five-foot-five or so. But he was "wiry"—strong with a lot of stamina. In retrospect, I don't know how he gained or maintained such good health given his lifestyle. Pap loved alcohol: beer, wine, liquor—*anything* with alcohol (though he never drank on the job). He would have a beer with his breakfast of grits, eggs, and bacon, which he cooked for himself on a small gas stove in a room he rented from Emory Heath, a man who ran a juke joint over in "the quarters," (a black section of town where most of the saw mill workers lived). Though my grandfather never drank, he and Pap were best friends. Granddaddy Council always chided Pap about his drinking and womanizing, but he knew Pap wouldn't change, and he knew it wouldn't change their friendship, either.

And Pap loved to eat. Sometimes his midday meal was a Pepsi and can of sardines. But sometimes in the winter, we would get a bushel of oysters and roast them over a fire built in an old oil drum behind the store. In the summer, we'd occasionally find an "abandoned" watermelon in a field beside one of the tobacco barns where we'd just delivered fuel oil.

Our family business consisted of a wide variety of products and services all aimed at meeting the needs of a small farming and logging community. There was a grocery store with a custom meat market; a "dry goods" section that sold clothing; a home appliance store; a farm supply section that sold feed, seeds, insecticides, and fertilizer; and an oil company that supplied gasoline, home heating oil, and fuel for curing tobacco. The store itself was fifty feet wide and one hundred feet long, but there were also several warehouses and a large oil storage facility. Pap and I worked together in each of those areas from the time I was very small until I graduated from college.

It is fair to say that my father, grandfather, and uncles, who were the "boss men" of the company, showed no partiality in assigning work for Pap and me. I was shown no favoritism as the scion of the company president, and Pap was considered as much a part of the family as I was. We did the manual labor. We dug holes in which to bury 500-gallon oil tanks (which got a lot easier as I got older and stronger). We loaded, transported, and unloaded tons of fertilizer and feed that came in 200-pound burlap bags. We delivered fuel oil to businesses, tobacco barns, and homes where we often had to pull 200 feet of rubber hose in rainstorms and across muddy fields. And any mishap, like a busted bag of fertilizer or an over-run oil tank, was just between us.

Pap was also a philosopher. Sometimes when we would have a break, we would sit on the feed and fertilizer sacks in the warehouse and he would tell me about life … and love.

"Womens is the ruination of a man. They'll make you do things you know 'gon mess you up, but you do 'em anyways wid no understandin' or carin' why you done it."

Given my youth and wealth of inexperience, Pap's ruminations on the opposite sex were extremely educational. I trusted his insight because he knew, in every sense of the word, a lot of women. Young women and older women, all sizes and shapes, would make a point of flirting with Pap when they came in the store. He would do what he called "shuck and jive," what we now call "talk trash," to them. Very often, the conversations ended with, "Awright then, I see ya tonight, darlin'." He was "smooth," as Pap liked to put it.

Pap had a family, though I never knew them well. His wife, Minnie Belle, had left him many years before I knew him, but they had several children together—four girls and a boy, I think. He never talked about them very much, though he did see them often. And Pap confessed to having other children by other women, but he never talked much about them either.

Minnie's family was there in Hallsboro. In fact, his brother-in-law, Reno Boone, was a frequent drinking buddy of Pap's, and from time to time they would be very congenial. Then, at other times, they would have disagreements that turned ugly.

One Monday morning, I was sweeping the floor in the office when my grandfather got a phone call from the sheriff's office. It seemed Pap and Reno had gotten into a fight over the weekend and both of them had been arrested. Pap had asked the deputy to call my grandfather so he could come and get him out of jail. My grandfather did go get Pap, but he also got Reno. He stood the bail for both of them. He said he needed both of them to unload a train car loaded with fertilizer.

That afternoon, I asked Pap about his confrontation with Reno, and he said it was about some girl they had "got up with" over at Heath's Place. Heath had called the sheriff, and Pap and Reno spent the rest of the weekend in the county jail.

"But I done hired me a lawyer. I gon' pay back the bail money to Mistah Dave. I gon' sue Reno."

"What are you suing Reno for?" I asked.

"'Sault," he answered calmly. "Mr. Greer say Reno done me damage so I can sue him."

"Mr. Greer is your lawyer?" I asked.

"Yep. Mine and Reno's."

Nothing ever came of that legal battle, and I don't think Pap ever had any real malice. The suing had just been for the money. So, the charges were dropped, and Reno and Pap remained friends.

⌒

The summer of 1964 was between my junior and senior year in college. I spent it working with Pap, much as we had worked for most of my life. I had read about all the turmoil of the Civil Rights Movement, but it still hadn't created much change in my life even as other college students were getting caught up in the fervor of the movement. It was the "Freedom Summer," but at my little Baptist college, not much was changing. And in Hallsboro, not much seemed to be changing either.

We had just finished putting in a tobacco curer for Mr. Seymour Clemmons on a typical hot, humid day in July, and Pap and I had not been back to the store all day. It was way past closing time when we finished our job, so I took Pap straight to Heath's Place. As we arrived at the juke joint, we saw a group gathered outside the front door. It was a small, wooden-frame building, about forty-by-forty feet, and relatively clean given the heavy traffic in and out. (I think it had a C sanitation grade, which allowed it to stay open.) Heath's Place didn't have a porch. Instead, the front door opened directly out on to a dirt area where some folks had set up wooden chairs under a chinaberry tree. Seated close to the tree was an old black man with an electric guitar plugged into a small amplifier. A long, yellow electrical cord ran from the amplifier and through a window on the side of the building.

I don't remember what he was playing, but it had that bluesy rhythm and twang that made you want to close your eyes, wrap your hands around a cold beer, and drift away to some place that didn't exist. There were people standing, some sitting on the ground, and some in the wooden chairs. There were men and women, old and young, and even a few children, all listening quietly. Some of them moved to the rhythm of the music, some sang unintelligible lyrics to themselves, but all eyes were on the bluesman.

Pap and I sat in the cab of the truck, listening to the music and looking at the tableau painted there before us. With the windows rolled down, we could smell the swamp: a soft, musky smell of wet mud mixed with bay leaves and wisteria. The heat of the day seemed to be lifted and wafted away on the wings of the bluesman's music and absorbed by the soft, stealthy approach of the night.

"Now, that boy can play that thing, cain't he?" said Pap.

"Yep, never heard anything like it," I said.

"That's them low-down blues like they plays down to where my brother stay, down in Socastee. It come from down in your soul and outta your fingers to the guitar strings. Ain't the kinda music most folks like, 'less they life been down a lotta bad road. You want a beer?"

"Yeah, I believe I do," I answered. I wasn't much of a beer drinker and Pap had never offered to provide such a beverage, so I was a little surprised and curious when he asked me.

"Come on, then," he said as he got out of the truck and headed into the place.

In all the years I had known Pap, he had never taken me into Heath's Place. I had always picked him up outside and then delivered him back in the same place.

"You sure it's alright for me to go in there?" I asked.

"You wid me, ain't ya?" he replied as he walked ahead of me to open the front door.

It is hard to describe how I felt as the only white face in a crowded room of black men. They all turned to look at me as I came in, but it became merely a glance when they saw I was with Pap. There was a constant loud hum of conversation, though they seemed to want to keep the conversation low enough that they could still hear the guitar music outside.

The bar itself was rudimentary to say the least. It was made of two wide, rough pine boards about twelve feet long placed on two fifty-gallon oil drums, one on each end. At one end was an assortment of liquor, mostly bourbon, rum, gin, and vodka. On the other end was a big galvanized tub of ice filled with cans of beer.

I recognized Emory Heath behind the bar. "Two beers," said Pap.

Heath brought two cans of beer and set them down on the bar in front of us. "That'll be a dollar," he said.

Pap looked at me and said, "Pay the man."

Surprised at Pap's lack of hospitality, I counted out a dollar's worth of change and then handed it to Heath.

"Come on over here," instructed Pap.

We sat down on a wooden bench set against the outside wall. "Now if I'd paid for them beers, you would have been my guest. You pay for 'em, you a customer just like me and you be treated just like me, not like some white boy from outside."

As we sat there drinking our beer, various customers would come over, pull up a chair, and talk to us. Usually, they addressed their comments to Pap, but some of them, who knew me, asked how my mother and father were, how college was, and generally acted as if I was just another customer.

After a short while, I left Pap with his friends and headed home. As I got in the truck, the bluesman was still playing, there was still a group around him, and Heath had turned the outside lights on so that the glow from the lights mixed with the evening mist that came up from the swamp to form a halo around the whole scene.

When I got home, the television was on in the living room. The evening news was about the continuing search for the killers of three civil rights workers in Mississippi and Lyndon Johnson's signing of the Civil Rights Act. I wondered if Mississippi and Hallsboro, North Carolina, were just different pictures of the same South. Or was there another South about which I was unaware?

c⁓

Pap's health began to deteriorate as he got older to the point where he could no longer do the physical labor he had done for so long. But because he had no health insurance, my father kept him on the payroll at the store so he could be on the company policy. Pap came in almost every day and swept the floors in the store and the warehouses, and he told stories to anybody who would listen.

When Pap died in 1976, the funeral service was held at a small church down in Horry County, South Carolina. My parents were the only white folks there. They sat with the family.

c⁓

Pap had a lot to do with how I came to view people of color. He allowed me to see beyond the public persona some black folks presented at the time, because that's what many thought they should do. That persona was not so much contrived as it had just evolved over generations. Pap was unique; I was able to see *him*, not just the "colored man" who worked at the store. He was a real person with, more or less, the same virtues and vices as other people. He introduced me to folks who let their public faces slide away, so I got to know them as people not stereotypes. I believe they got to know me in the same way. Pap was as much an educator as any professor I had in college. But, beyond his role as educator, he was my friend. That's what I remember most.

Fish in the Ditch

I was on a solitary ramble down one of my favorite dirt roads when I saw Leon Boone fishing in a ditch. It's not unusual to see folks fishing from a bridge across a small swamp run or creek, however, Leon was fishing in a ditch: a water channel only about five feet wide and four feet deep. It ran from Bogue Swamp and through a culvert under the old dirt road just down from my house.

I had not seen Leon in quite a while. We grew up in the same community and he lived not far from me, though our paths never really seemed to cross. But since we knew each other, I figured he wouldn't think it strange if I stopped to visit with him out in the edge of the swamp.

After I pulled my old pickup truck over to the side of the road, I started walking down to where he was perched on a white plastic bucket turned upside down. Leon wore a pair of cut-off blue jeans shorts and a T-shirt. No shoes. He was far enough off the road that the shade from the cypress trees gave him some respite from the hot summer sun.

As I walked up he said, "Hey, William." (People who have known me since childhood still call me William.)

"Hey, Leon. Haven't seen you in a while. Whatcha doin'?"

"Drownin' worms," he replied.

"Not many fish, huh?" I asked.

"Nope. But I don't expect to catch any outta this ditch anyhow."

"Whatcha doin' out here with a fishin' pole then?"

"Wastin' time," he said. "There's a cold Mountain Dew in that ice chest over there. Get you one of 'em and have a seat on that stump."

I did as I was instructed. After I had struggled to get my long, lanky, and aging frame situated on the stump, I realized how quiet the swamp was. The moss hanging on the cypress limbs barely moved in the easy breeze. Somewhere in the distance, I could hear birds chirping. The water in the ditch was so slow-moving it didn't make a sound. The sweet, delicate smell of the bay bushes mingled with the sour smell of swamp water and mud.

As if he'd been reading my mind, Leon said, "Peaceful out here, ain't it?"

"Yep. I kinda like this," I answered.

"Me too. That's the real reason I come out here. Don't nobody hardly ever come by and I can just forget 'bout all the bad stuff and think about the good without any interruption."

I sensed I was one of those interruptions, so I started to get up from the stump. "Well, I just thought I'd stop and see you a minute and ..."

"Aw, sit down, son. You ain't no interruption. Just sit on that stump a while. Sometimes it's sharing good times that makes 'em good times. Don't say nothin'; just listen to the Lord's creation."

So, I tried to "listen to the Lord's creation." What I heard was the silence. In that silence, I began to think the way Leon had said he did when he came out to fish in the ditch. I began to "think on all the good stuff." I thought about how lucky I was to have had so much good in my life and so little really bad. I thought about all the opportunities I'd had to do so many things, meet so many people, see so many places. Then I thought, "How lucky am I to be able to come to a place like this, to renew my acquaintance with an old friend, to find a spot more therapeutic than any session held in a psychiatrist's office?"

My reverie was shortened as Leon rose from his seat on the bucket and began to gather himself and his fishing equipment to leave. As he did so, I noted, "You don't even have a worm on that hook! How'd you expect to catch anything?"

Leon laughed as he said, "Oh, I didn't 'spect to catch nothin'. I just needed to give myself an excuse to come out here. Now, if you really want to catch fish, come on down to the lake with me tomorrow and we'll do some real fishin'. I'll come pick you up at your house 'bout dusk dark or mornin' light, whichever you want."

I thanked him for the offer but said I wasn't much of a fisherman.

"Then you come back down here and fish any time," he said as he laughed and waved goodbye.

A professor told me one time that creativity is being able to express dreams. But first you gotta see the dreams. Leon showed me how to see dreams just by sitting on the side of a ditch with a friend and listening to the Lord's creation. As I got back in my truck, I thought about how my afternoon, non-fishing experience had been time well wasted.

John Paul and the Chicken Auction

*I*t was not good weather for a chicken auction that day. Gray clouds covered the sky over the parking lot, but a chorus of caged roosters proclaimed the hidden sunrise. John Paul Smith stood in the midst of at least a hundred cages filled with all kinds of poultry. "People will come. You watch what I tell you," he announced.

And they did come. All kinds of people arrived in the parking lot across the street from Gurganus Farm Supply in Whiteville. They unloaded cages from truck beds and all kinds of trailers, as well as the trunks and back seats of automobiles. They placed the ever-expanding flock in a winding row that led to three folding tables that constituted a makeshift auction block on the east side of the lot.

Just to the left of the auction tables was a smaller table set up to accommodate the bookkeeping necessary for an auction. (An auction has to have a permit from the state, and an inspector from the North Carolina Department of Agriculture must be present.) Behind the temporary office was a small food concession cart selling hot dogs and soft drinks. Even at seven o'clock in the morning, they had plenty of business.

John Paul (called by both names as dictated by Southern tradition) moved around the scene, talking comfortably with the sellers and prospective buyers. He knew many of the people by name. He had grown up in Columbus County, just south of the Bladen-Columbus county line. He seemed to fit right in. He was dressed in a neat T-shirt and a pair of khaki shorts, his feet were ensconced in the traditional work boots common in every rural community. In his late forties at the time, John Paul was a man who loved food. And it showed.

He watched the preliminary to the auction with the optimism that had sustained him all his young life. A puff of wind blew the chickens' feathers as they pecked at grains of corn and clucked. Having grown up on a farm, John Paul was extremely knowledgeable about chickens as well as other farm inhabitants. His farm background had taken him into the hog business for a while, but when the old Gurganus Milling Company building had been put up for sale, John Paul saw an opportunity. There were few independent farm supply businesses in the state and even fewer who did custom milling for animal feed.

"The town was about to condemn the property," he recalled recently. "They told us we had thirty days to improve it or it'd be condemned." The structure is now sturdy, but it still maintains some elements of its past, including a covered wooden porch across the front with sacks of feed stacked neatly against the wall.

Behind the store are several large grain storage bins. "We buy grain from the farmers. Some we sell and some we use to mix feed," the young entrepreneur observed as we sat on the auction stand. "We still cater to the farmer who wants things his way, who may or may not want a whole tractor-trailer load of feed and wants a particular mix. That makes us unique. We're not a one-size-fits-all company."

That down-home approach is evident in the store itself. There are bags of feed stacked across the floor of the building. There are bags of dog food and cat food, chicken feed, bird feed, horse feed, hog feed, goat feed, cow feed, and even some fish feed and deer feed. There are also several bags of fertilizer on one side of the building. The walls are lined with insecticides, tin and galvanized buckets, vet needs and medicines, and just about anything else a farmer would want, as well as small gardening tools and an array of tack for horses. All the different smells give a unique aromatic rush to the visitor when he opens the door.

Over on one side of the store, light from a small heat lamp peeks over the stacks of feed. The sound of chicks ("biddies") murmuring to each other escapes from the small, open-topped cages placed on the floor and warmed by the light. It's a nostalgic scene, a diorama plucked from the memories of many of the people who visit the store. How many remember witnessing that same scene years ago in their own barns or chicken houses, or even in their mother's kitchen on cold winter days? It's an image that probably generates a lot of sales.

It's that same nostalgia that may have stirred folks to spend their money at the auction as well. One man said, "I just came to see what was goin' on and got so caught up in everything, I bought twenty chickens and a rooster. I had to talk John Paul into keepin' 'em 'til I could go home and build a chicken house. Now, ain't that somethin'?"

That man's sentiment was typical of the folks who gathered that cloudy Saturday for the auction. The interest in chickens cut across all social lines. In addition to farmers, several Hispanic families stood next to some retired folks who had just moved from Pennsylvania to the beach. Even a few young urban types, neophyte auction-goers, stood in the cool morning air, eating hot dogs as they moved from pen to pen to look more closely at the chickens.

As we watched people stroll through the rows of pens, John Paul laughed when he related, "I had a young lady ask me one time what was the difference between the chickens that gave eggs she ate for breakfast and the ones that laid the eggs that hatched chicks. She didn't believe me when I told her the same chickens laid both eggs."

When I asked him why he thought the auction sales had gone so well, John Paul said, "Some people want to raise chickens and make a little money. A few want 'em for food. Some want 'em for eggs. And some want 'em just to have around. They can buy 'em fairly cheap compared to other things."

Shortly after seven o'clock, the auction began. John Paul stood behind the auctioneer. Sometimes he would bid, sometimes he would comment on a particular pen of birds.

The auctioneer kept the sale moving along with the familiar chant. Ironically, this man who had been the auctioneer since John Paul first started hosting the sales had never previously auctioned livestock of any kind. He was an automobile auctioneer who converted to chickens.

The sale continued with few interruptions; even the rain held off. People continued to unload poultry; hot dog sales increased as the morning went on; buyers loaded their purchases into whatever conveyance they had; and the cluck of chickens and crowing of roosters trumpeted across the parking lot and down the streets of Whiteville.

John Paul Smith stood in the midst of it all, supervising an activity that was an incongruity, even a paradox, of time and place. He was a young man succeeding in a business many saw as a part of the past. He succeeded because he adapted to new markets. He was innovative while building on the appeal of the past.

⁓

It wasn't too long ago that the income of most North Carolinians was tied to agriculture. That has changed as the technical and service industry has become a bigger part of our economy. But John Paul has been creative and innovative and, most importantly, as he says, "I like what I'm doing."

In looking at his achievements in the farm supply business, it may be appropriate to reflect on something another entrepreneur, Henry Ford, said: "Business is never so healthy as when, like a chicken, it must do a certain amount of scratching around for what it gets."

H.J. White and the Mules

*N*othing marks the transition of Southern culture, from the pastoral image of family farms to the New South of corporate agriculture, more than the rise and fall of the mule; and no one followed or assisted that transition more than Henry James (H.J.) White Jr. He was part of a prominent Bladen County family here in North Carolina whose family business was selling horses and mules at a time when such a business was essential to the community's economy. H.J completely belied the old stereotype of the horse trader: the slick, fast-talking shyster. Instead, he was well-educated, having graduated from Wake Forest College, and an astute businessman. He gained part of his business experience after he came back home from college and got involved in the family business. That was a time when the mule business was an essential part of agriculture, kinda like tractor and combine companies are now.

H.J. and I first met when I went to work at Boys Home in 1966. He had his family's horse and mule sale barn in Bladenboro, about a twenty-minute drive from the campus at Lake Waccamaw. I had my own horse there, and occasionally people would donate a horse to the home. Usually, the animal donated was the kind that could not be sold (sick to near death, lame, too high spirited, etc.), or the donor was able to get a better financial return by giving the horse to Boys Home and claiming a tax deduction than he could get by selling it. Since neither I nor the Home had a horse trailer at that time, I would ask H.J. to come and look at a horse, take whatever price he would give, and bring his trailer to pick up the horse. There was not a lot of real horse trading going on, more like disposal of unusable property.

Over the years, we got to be friends, despite an age difference of almost four decades. Back in about 1967, the Lake Waccamaw Lions Club decided to build a horse show ring on the Boys Home farm. Proceeds from shows were divided equally between the home and the Lions Club. H.J. and I worked together to organize the shows, which were very successful. Later, the home put in a 50,000-square-foot covered arena.

H.J. was a great promoter. He helped organize the Border Belt Horseman's Association, which generated many local horse shows—and created a market for the horses he sold. It was his idea that he and I should publish a magazine to promote the growing local interest in horses. So, we started a magazine called *Horseman's Digest*. We bought a small mobile home for our office and placed it in front of the sale barn in Bladenboro. I was the editor and co-publisher, and I immediately began traveling over North and South Carolina, Virginia, Tennessee, and Georgia to sell advertisements and write stories. In about a year, we had nearly 5,000 subscribers, but we weren't making a lot of money. So, when an offer came to sell the magazine to another horse publication down in Mississippi, we sold it, and I went back to work full-time at Boys Home.

The most fascinating part of my time as editor of the magazine was not directly related to the publication. Since my office was in front of H.J.'s sale barn, I got to meet and interact with a lot of horse people, more accurately, I got to see *H.J.* interact with horse people.

H.J. was much like his customers. He was amiable, but he could get really serious talking about horses and mules. He was a short man who dressed in western attire complete with a cattleman's hat, which was more conservative than a cowboy hat but nevertheless distinctive. He always wore a pair of black cowboy boots that shined, even in the barnyard. And he was an excellent salesman.

Even as late as the late 1960s and early '70s, a lot of folks in Bladen County still used mules on their farms, usually in addition to their tractors, and some folks used mules to plow their gardens. Many of those people were H.J.'s customers.

There was one local gentleman who came by the barn very late on a Saturday afternoon. The man, of undetermined but late vintage, lived not too far down the road and drove his mule and wagon into town almost every Saturday. I'd always see him driving by dressed in his denim overalls and shirt, with a John Deere cap and cowboy boots. On one such afternoon, H.J. and I were closing up to go home for the day, and we heard the sound of a mule and wagon coming down the street. We turned to see Calvin, driving his hitch and singing at the top of his lungs, "Gonna lay down my burden, down by the riverside, down by the riverside, down by the riverside ...." Just as he pulled up in front of H.J. and me, he pulled back on the cotton rope he used for reins, said, "Whoa!" and he promptly fell out of the wagon. H.J. and I rushed over to see if he was hurt.

H.J. asked, "Are you alright?"

The obviously intoxicated gentleman responded as he brushed dirt from his bib overalls, "Oh, I'm alright. Just when I git to where I'm goin', I just go ahead and git right on outta the wagon."

The old gentleman had come to trade in his mule for a younger model. But H.J. would not do business with anybody in such an intoxicated state. He told him to get back on the wagon (literally) and he would drive him home. So, H.J. got in the wagon with his potential customer and then drove the mule and wagon about two miles down the road to Calvin's home and dropped him (literally) on the porch. I had followed behind them in the darkness with the lights flashing on my truck. I'm sure we made an interesting sight.

The thing that was most reflective of H.J. White's character that evening was not so much how he'd refused to take advantage of the man's drunken condition, nor that he'd taken him safely home. The most telling part was how, after we'd gotten there, he and I unhitched the mule from the wagon, put the mule in the barn, and fed the animal. A real horseman never neglects his animal—nor anybody else's.

Now, having said all that, I wouldn't want anybody to think that H.J. was not a shrewd horse and mule trader. Sometime later that spring, a fellow named Leon Henry came by the barn, wanting to trade mules. He told H.J., "Had that mule a long time. Near 'bout since I was a boy. Daddy owned 'im. I inherited 'im from Daddy. 'Bout all I ever do with 'im is plow my garden every year. Now, he cain't do that, so I need to trade 'im."

H.J. said, "Well, I might have just what you need. Bought him from a fella over in Lumberton. He plows good, no ailments, a good keeper."

H.J. went back in the barn and brought out a big, black mare mule. (Mules have gender, but they cannot breed.) He had one of the men who worked at the barn harness the mule and hitch her to a "drag." Then the barn hand stood on the drag and drove the mule around the area in front of the barn. The mule never balked, just pulled her load steadily, her head moving up and down rhythmically, responding easily to the reins as they changed direction.

Leon and H.J. watched the presentation without comment. Finally, H.J. asked Leon if he wanted to work the mule himself. Leon said he did and then took the reins from the barn hand, stood on the drag, and drove the mule around the barn yard.

The outcome of the demonstration was that Leon traded his old mule for the younger one plus a little "to boot." The old mule was put in the barn and the black mule was loaded on Leon's trailer. H.J. turned to me and said, "He'll be back and want to trade for his old mule after he gets his garden plowed."

I asked, "What makes you so sure?"

"I been trading that mule now for about five or six years. She is just as good as she looked just now. But when Leon gets that mule to his garden, that mule will give him a time. That mule's been well cared for here. She likes it here. She works well here. But when she goes off somewhere else, she wants to come back to this barn. She'll work Leon hard; she'll want to run off with the plow, step across the rows. Long as she's walking away from Leon's barn, she'll do pretty good, but when he turns her around toward the barn, that mule's ready to go home. Leon'll get plowing done though."

About a month or so later, I saw Leon drive up in front of the office trailer. Sure enough, he wanted to trade the mule back for his daddy's old mule. I watched out the window as the exchange took place. After Leon left, I went over to the barn and asked H.J. if he didn't feel bad about trading that mule to Leon.

"Nope," he answered. "His old mule couldn't plow his garden. The black mule could. He got his garden plowed and still got to keep his daddy's mule. I got the little bit of boot and my mule back. It's kinda like he rented that black mule for the spring."

I watched H.J. practice the art of mule trading for many years. I learned a lot—the feed and care, sales presentation, and how to determine what the customers really wanted. But one of the things I enjoyed most about my association with H.J. White was his ability to tell a good story. He had many opportunities to share that ability as almost every day, folks would come to the old sale barn and just linger. They wanted to see the horses and mules, but they also loved to hear H.J. tell his stories.

I went with him many times down to the monthly sale and auction at Bennettsville, South Carolina. I remember the man named Max who ran the sale. He was as colorful a character as H.J. Maybe that's why H.J. loved to tell this story:

Max ran the auction down to Bennettsville. Now, he had a lot of those traits attributed to horse traders, some true and some not so true. He was not above selling an animal that had received more than the usual preparation for the sale, but he never flat out misrepresented the animal to the buyer.

The sale at Bennettsville was Max's creation and was unlike any you will ever find anywhere else. He sold not only livestock but furniture, wagons, saddles, and an occasional household appliance. Not all at the same time, of course. The first Monday of the month was his sale date, and it took all day to dispose of his consignments.

I [H.J.] used to go down there about dusk in time for the mule sale. This would be followed by grade [unregistered] horses, then the registered horses. Sometimes it would be almost midnight before the registered horses would sell, but the crowd would still be there.

Max was a master salesman. He would sit up on the counter of the sale ring with the auctioneer, his legs dangling down into the sale pen, and he'd hold a riding crop in his hand. Every once in a while, he'd calm the crowd by slapping that crop against the wall and advising all the non-buying spectators to go outside to do their drinking.

Max's prowess as a salesman was tested one night during the mule auction as two matched sorrel mules were brought into the ring. Everybody wanted them, so the bidding was fast and high; and in a relatively short time, a man from Clio bought the pair for a pretty good price. Max praised the man for his astute mule sense and then ran the next mule in.

In about twenty minutes, the man came running back into the barn, pulled Max down from the counter and began to strike him while giving him an ol' time cussin'. It seemed the mules were blind, and the man had not intended to buy blind mules.

The reason I think Max was more than your ordinary horse trader is the fact that he convinced the man that the mules were only temporarily blind and would be able to see clearly right after the first frost. Max was more than a horse trader; he was a politician.

H.J. was a pretty good politician himself.

Part 3
THE WILD WIND OF ENTERTAINMENT

The Wild Wind of Entertainment

Music has been such a big part of my life, I can't decide whether it has been the accompaniment or the inspiration. Did I write the music or did I just sing along? And while music hasn't been my entire life, it wouldn't be much of a life without it.

I grew up in a musical family where every gathering included some kind of musical performance by almost every member. My Great Grandfather Flynn played a fiddle for local dances near Red Bug. My Grandfather Thompson could play just about any instrument "by ear." He played the fiddle for local dances, and he would listen to songs on the radio, then immediately play them on the piano or clarinet.

I was going to be a music major in college until my professor and I mutually agreed that, since music theory was a requirement for the degree, I should look for another line of work. But I still stayed in the music department as part of the touring choir for four years. During that time, I broadened my musical interests to include classical music and opera.

My sister and I grew up singing in the church choirs, of course; but when our Aunt Mary Lee died, she left us a huge pile of sheet music. We went through it all: the syncopated rhythms of ragtime in the '20s, the big band sounds of the '30s, and especially all the songs of World

War II; the songs that could briefly beat out the sounds of bombs and the screams of war. They were the songs of a life, a home worth fighting for. Remember "The House I Live In"?

When we went off to college in the '60s, Linda played guitar, I played rhythm instruments (bongos, tambourines, and the like), and we sang folk music for anybody who would listen—especially anybody who would pay us. We were inspired by the The Kingston Trio; Peter, Paul and Mary; Joan Baez; and all the other "folk revivalists" of the period.

Out of our folk music interest grew an appreciation for "bluegrass." Somewhere along the way, bluegrass lost its "hillbilly" image and evoked the heritage of the mountains and hollers, the mill villages and tobacco fields that were so much a part of who we were as North Carolinians. Bluegrass spoke of back porches and pig pickin's, barbecue and hush puppies, coon hunts on cold nights and fishing on reed-covered banks.

Even as my musical interests expanded, I was never far from my eastern North Carolina roots. I still listened to the Grand Ol' Opry, the honky-tonk sounds of Earnest Tubb, the silky voice of Patsy Cline, and the plaintive wail of Hank Williams.

At the same time, another Williams boy kept tugging me back home to the beaches, the parties, the days in the sun. Maurice Williams was his name; and the Zodiacs, the Tams, and the Embers made rhythm and blues into a special sound called "beach music." Beach music is more than just music. It's a lifestyle unique to the Carolinas; a lifestyle that cuts across race and social and economic backgrounds. When "My Girl" is wafting out over the sand dunes, the soft breeze from the sea is moving the sea grass, and the moonlight is reflected on waves as they lap the shore, it can feel as if life has no boundaries and youth lasts forever.

Soon after I graduated from college, I became the director of a boys' choir at what was then Boys Home of North Carolina. I tried to incorporate as many different kinds of music as I thought the boys should appreciate, including some patriotic songs they needed to learn. I think they liked the folk songs and the patriotic songs and even some of the Broadway stuff. Classical? Not so much.

The music of my life is like a multi-layered cake. Each layer is separate, unique, and wonderful. Put together, it's a rich, delicious mixture that can't be duplicated or consumed all at once.

I tried to think up some appropriate words, mine or somebody else's, to sum up what music has meant to my life. I concluded that trying to explain an appreciation for music and its role in a person's life is like music itself; a composer can put words and notes on paper, but to really express the emotion, he has to feel it, play it, sing it, or share it so, the listener can feel the same emotion. That's the art of music ... and of writing. That emotional connection is so ephemeral, only a few can really grasp it.

I'm still working on it.

I Want to Hear It Again

No matter how hard we try, how much attention we pay to details, how much research we do, or how committed we are, we can never create another first time. By definition, a first time means it can't be repeated. As I get older, I often wish I could recreate some of the most momentous moments of my life. Some I can't repeat because I don't remember them: my first steps, my first words. Some I don't want to repeat, in fact, some I'd just as soon forget.

Still, as I get older, I naturally reflect on my past. In doing so, I have found there is one recurring theme for me: music. Almost every aspect of my life has been influenced in some way by music. Some of those times I was a performer and sometimes I was a listener. But in every case, the first time I had a specific musical experience, it would affect how I proceeded from then on. And although I can't hear or sing songs for the first time again, I can recall the feelings I had in that moment, and the time and place in which I had them.

I want to hear again for the first time the sound of a country band with a steel guitar, playing in a room so filled with smoke that it looks like the place is on fire. I want to watch again for the first time those non-dancers who simply move their feet (and whatever other parts of their body still work) to the beat of the music. I want to listen for the first time to a song about home and railroads and lost love and pickup trucks and Mama.

I want to hear again for the first time the clear voice of a young soprano learning Puccini's "Un Bel Di, Vedremo" from *Madame Butterfly*. I want to hear that aria as it rings down the hall of the college music building, mixing with the sounds of a violin and an oboe, and other instruments and other voices, to form a beautiful cacophony. I want to the hear the pipe organ in the chapel as it pushes out Bach's *Toccata and Fugue* across the campus on a cold winter's night, accompanying young lovers who hold hands as they walk down the brick walkways that weave between classroom buildings.

I want to hear again for the first time the sea breeze that blows across the sand dunes and lifts the easy rhythm of "My Girl" to the outdoor pavilion where couples dance, their fingers barely touching, their Weejuns sliding across the wooden dance floor. I want to hear the youthful laughter. I want to feel the sense of time and place created there that will be transfered to the next generation and the next, and become a part of our Southern heritage.

I want to hear for the first time the sound of a worn-out guitar playing the real blues, the kind that bursts and ripples and weeps and shouts and whispers from the soul of the black man who plays it on the dirt patio of a juke joint where I'm not supposed to be. I want to hear his voice as it sheds a lifetime of struggle and acquiescence at the feet of those like him who have shared that struggle and understand that acquiescence.

I want to hear again for the first time, the blending of choir voices: a small country-church choir that sings those old hymns sung from memory, accompanied by a pianist who plays "by ear" on an upright piano with chipped keys; a choir of young boys lifted from home situations where they were abused and neglected but, through music, are now lifted above their pasts; a choir of small children, myself among them, each singing their own version of "I Wonder As I Wander" to an audience of family members. And, yes, I want to hear again for the first time the applause of the audience when I sang my first solo as a member of my high school chorus after the football coach, who had previously viewed me as mostly inadequate, said, "Damn, boy! You can sing!"

I want to hear again for the first time the comfortable, magical blend of voices and a beat-up old guitar as my sister and I sang the folk songs of the '60s to any group that would pay us, even if the pay was just a meal.

Time doesn't dim the memory of such things. Each of these sounds is indelibly imprinted in my mind, and I can recall every single one as clearly as if it happened just yesterday.

That's a good thing, I guess, since I can never recreate the first time.

Miss Annie Made a Difference

You hear a lot of talk today about making a difference. Most of the time it is about doing something in the future, something positive, something different from the past. That's good, and I'm all for it, but sometimes we forget to look at what made a positive difference in the past.

In keeping with my personal slogan, "Everything in the world is personal," I have to look at the past through a personal lens to those people who made a difference in my life and, certainly, in the lives of so many of my contemporaries.

If we asked a hundred people to name the most influential people in their lives, I bet almost every one of them would include a teacher on the list … probably more than one. That would certainly be the case for me.

From first grade until high school graduation, I attended the same school in Hallsboro. Ours was a small, rural community where you had the same classmates every year. Not many students came or left. Neither did the teachers. I had some of the same teachers my mother had learned from when she went to school there. One of those teachers was Miss Annie Elkins.

Miss Annie taught music and English. Through the years, she taught English to different classes, but she taught music to everybody

… every year. She taught in the classroom and also directed the school chorus. There was a chorus for everybody. Then in high school, we had the "glee club."

Glee club was nothing like the wild performances you see on "Glee," the television program, apart from the audition process and after-school rehearsals. Our glee club was much more formal, much more structured, much more *dignified*. Dignity was a big deal as far as Miss Annie was concerned. Strongly religious and quite old-fashioned, Miss Annie insisted that all of the choral groups, including glee club, rehearse and perform on risers. Talking was forbidden during rehearsals, and choreography was certainly not allowed. We didn't even move to the rhythm of the music.

The music we sang in glee club was traditional, even classical, much of it religious and a lot of it patriotic. When we learned a new song, Miss Annie would make mimeographed copies of the music. (For those who don't know about mimeographs, look it up. It was a bulky process and the ink had a unique smell.) She tried to teach us the basics of how to read music, but usually we just sang the parts over and over until we got it the way she wanted. The only music book I remember using, other than an occasional piece with piano accompaniment, was *The Golden Book of Favorite Songs*.

The Golden Book of Favorite Songs wasn't just for chorus. Back then, we had a general assembly at least once a week, where every student filed into the auditorium. The principal would say a prayer, and then the student body would recite the Pledge of Allegiance to the flag of the United States of America, sing a song from *The Golden Book*, and listen to a short speech. I don't remember the speeches, but I remember the prayer, the pledge, and the songs.

And Miss Annie Elkins was there, a vital part of it, every day for all twelve years.

I don't know how old Miss Annie actually was. She had always just been *old*. Age is not relevant to a small child, old is old. She was a very tiny woman—barely five-feet tall and thin. Her hair was always gray and was always in a bun. At one point, the boys in the woodwork shop made her a stand to conduct from, but she refused to use it. She said it was our responsibility to see her, not for her to see us. The most distinctive memory I have of Miss Annie teaching us to sing was her reaching on top of a student's head and pulling a strand of hair up to indicate they needed to sing on pitch.

⌒

Now, here's the personal part. All through school, I was a nerd. I was skinny, wore glasses, and had a very noticeable overbite. I made good grades, but I was too small to play athletics, so I was the scorekeeper and the "stringer" for the local newspaper. My singular distinction was my voice. Even when I was little, I loved to sing. Miss Annie thought I had a good voice, so she would spend extra time working with me. She would assign me solos, and I would always sing in ensemble groups. And when we had school plays, she would ensure I had a singing role. She even had me sing the National Anthem for a meeting of area teachers one time and introduced me as one of her best students. I was flattered, but one of my buddies burst my bubble by whispering that, "In the land of the blind, the one-eyed man is king." Still, her special attention gave me confidence and self-esteem I would have never had otherwise.

I never attained fame or fortune in the music field, but I was fortunate enough to appear in a wide range of venues over the years (either as a speaker, master of ceremonies, or performer) that allowed me to use the musical talents Miss Annie had honed so early on.

⌒

Looking out from the stage over an audience at a spectacular canyon on a late autumn afternoon, the sun shines on the rim, casting a shadow on the sandy floor. It stretches like a tan carpet. Dotted with an indistinct brush are the green juniper and chinaberry trees, and an occasional rocky mound formed by the winds that blow continuously across west Texas. Somewhere in those rocks and trees remain the ghosts of the Kiawah and Comanche who lived there for centuries before the white man. Maybe they're listening tonight under this cloudless blue sky.

1979 at the Pioneer Amphitheater: the original site for the Paul Green drama, *Texas*. The outdoor stage was set on the floor of the Palo Duro Canyon in the Texas panhandle. I was honored to sing with the Amarillo Symphony Orchestra in a tribute to the North Carolinian who wrote the play.

A soft breeze replaces the wind, a full orchestra behind me. Oh, how I wish Miss Annie could see me now.

Arthur Smith: Mr. Music Man

*I*n 1967, shortly after I went to work at Boys Home, we began what was to become a tradition for the Boys Home choir. Right after Thanksgiving, we would leave the campus at Lake Waccamaw, down in the southeastern part of North Carolina, and begin visiting every television station across the state—plus a few in South Carolina and Virginia—to perform Christmas music as part of the annual fundraising effort. This was before videotape recording was available, so every program was live. And we didn't have a bus, so we traveled in three station wagons.

The boys, all between the ages of ten and fifteen, loved being in the choir. They got to travel, meet all kinds of people, receive applause for their performances—and get out of school.

At that time, every local station had a morning show that featured local garden clubs, performers, and any other programing that fell under the title of "community service." The Federal Communication Commission required that local stations present such programing as a part of licensing requirements, so they were always happy to have us.

It wasn't long, however, before videotaping became available and we were able to do full-length (thirty-minute) programs at one station, then physically take the original tape to all the other stations. I would take the tape to one station, wait for them to "dub" a copy, then proceed to the next one.

In the early 1970s, we began taping our Christmas show in the studios of WSOC-TV in Charlotte. Since we had to drive three hours to Charlotte, we usually scheduled our taping for some time in the afternoon. As it happened, a fellow named Arthur Smith and his band, the Crackerjacks, always taped their weekly show just before us. Arthur Smith was an icon in the music business. He had begun his television career across town at WBT-TV, recorded several songs that became hits, written songs for other people, and provided management for some of the most famous singers in the country. He became known as "the Music Man," a title he wore for many years. Since we always got to the studio a little early, Arthur and his band would be taping when we got there.

Fred Thompson (no kin), a newsman at the station, was a mutual friend of Arthur's and mine, and had introduced us. I was familiar with Arthur since he and his group were popular on the radio at that time and they had performed at the school auditorium in Hallsboro. I was impressed, but Arthur had made me feel welcome right away. We immediately became friends.

Arthur had a recording studio on Old Monroe Road that was a state-of-the-art facility at that time, and a lot of nationally-known performers would come to his studio to record. Over the years, if I was in Charlotte for any reason, I would go by his studio to say hello and, frankly, just to see who might be there. George Hamilton IV was often there and I got to know him as well. I remembered his first hit song, "A Rose and a Baby Ruth," from my high school days, but for me his most memorable song was "Abilene." My sister and I had made that song part of our repertoire when we sang folk songs during our college days.

On one of my visits to Arthur's studio, George was there. After some conversation, he agreed to appear on one of our Boys Home choir programs. In the course of any television taping session, there are always long waits while producers review what has already been recorded, or for various other reasons. During one of those breaks at WSOC, I mentioned the fact that my sister and I used to sing "Abilene." He jokingly said he didn't remember getting any royalties from our performances. Nonetheless, he asked if I wanted to sing that song with him. Of course, I did. So we sang it right then and there, behind the scenes at the station, as if we'd been singing together for years.

Over the years, George became a friend and major supporter of Boys Home, and we stayed in touch. He became known as "the Ambassador of Country Music" because of his very successful tours of Europe. But for me, he is best remembered for our impromptu duet in the old studio there at WSOC.

Starting in about 1975, I began traveling, singing, and emceeing as a result of my association with the Miss North Carolina pageants around the state, and the exposure I gained from my involvement with Boys Home. Someone from another state would invite me to a performance, so I'd travel out to them. This expanded into convention performances as I became associated with Talent Network, a talent agency in Greensboro. I was most active in the late '70s and early '80s, though I still continue to travel for engagements to this day.

In the course of my traveling around the country, singing for anybody who would have me, some folks said, "You ought to consider singing professionally." I always figured that "professionally" meant full-time performing, making a living at it. As much as I liked performing, I realized there were a lot of people much more talented than me who were barely making it from day-to-day. Still, I really gave the idea of lot of thought. So, in 1979, during one of my visits to Arthur's studio, I asked him what he thought about my prospects. He said, "Why don't you make an audition tape? I'll tell you what I think." Well, I couldn't afford the studio time at Arthur's, so I came back home and taped some songs in the little studio that my friend Alford Hayes had out near Whiteville.

When I got the tape completed, I took it to Arthur in Charlotte. He said he'd call me in a few days. A couple of weeks went by and I hadn't heard from him, so I called him. He told me to come by to see him the next time I was in Charlotte. I made it a point to "happen to be in Charlotte" the following week.

I went to the studio and Arthur suggested we go to lunch at a little café just down the road. I was anxious to know what he thought. But when he finally told me, I didn't know how to respond. Arthur was a Southern gentleman. He was very straight-forward in his assessment of my voice, but he tried to be as gentle as he could in telling me I didn't have what it took.

He said, "Son, you got a good voice—clear, good tone—but it's not what we call 'commercial.'" Arthur's strong "country accent" was redolent of his South Carolina upbringing. He cultivated it because it helped his audience identify with him and his music.

"You see," he continued, "you got to have something that makes your voice so different, if somebody hears you on the radio, they automatically know it's your voice. That don't necessarily mean it's got to be good, just different. Some of the folks that come in my studio sound like they been smoking too many cigarettes, but they write original songs and they sell it with their voice. Plus, they got good managers."

I guess Arthur could see my disappointment. He went on to encourage me to continue singing. "Just do it 'cause you want to," he said.

After we finished our lunch, I went on over to talk with the folks at WSOC about plans for doing a remote taping of our Boys Home Christmas show. As soon as I walked in the lobby of the station, the receptionist told me Arthur had called and wanted to talk to me right away.

I went into a little side office and called Arthur. He said, "Bill, when I got back to the studio, I had a call from somebody you might be interested in working with. He is looking for somebody to sing regularly on a nationally telecast show. I told him I might know just the fella. I played him your tape. He thinks your voice will fit right in with his kind of music. It's called 'contemporary gospel.' You think you'd be interested?"

I told him I didn't know what contemporary gospel was. I knew about Southern gospel and black gospel, but I wasn't familiar with contemporary gospel. I asked him what it was.

"Well, it's kind of a cross between pop, maybe a little bit rock and roll, a little bit of Southern gospel, and maybe a little bit of traditional sacred music. I think your voice would fit in there. 'Course now the catch to this is, I got to give him an answer right now. I'll act as your agent and make sure it pays good."

I thought about the offer. I was excited about the opportunity this presented: singing for a living. But it was a big leap. I had a family to support. I had a regular job with a regular salary. Could I give that up on the chance I could be successful in singing music I wasn't familiar with? I was reluctant to take on so much unknown.

"Who would I be working with?" I asked.

"Well, I can't tell you that until you tell me you're interested," he said. Arthur was a Southern business man, gently persuasive.

Could I go to work for some unknown person singing unfamiliar music? I decided to turn down the offer.

⌒

As I write this book and look back at all the decisions I've made over the years, I know now that some were good and some were bad. But I believe my decision not to work for Jim and Tammy Faye Bakker over at the PTL Network was a good one.

Ola Lewis Brought Music to the Courthouse

When I think about music at the county courthouse, about the only thing that comes to mind is somebody singing the national anthem for a special occasion. But Ola Lewis didn't limit her thinking.

Back in the fall of 2008, Ola had recently become the Resident Superior Court Judge of Judicial District 13-B, which includes her home County of Brunswick. Ola decided that since the new Brunswick County Courthouse, where she often presided, was the "people's courthouse," it should be a place to celebrate the county's people, their culture, and the collective personality of the area and its heritage. To Ola, it naturally followed that music was the medium to accomplish all of that.

Coming to such a decision was "natural" for Ola, because music and the arts had always been such a big part of her life. "I thought of being a ballerina when I was growing up," she told me as we sat in her chambers in the courthouse. "The pursuit of the arts is not only a great path for self-expression, it is also great training for life's journey—even if that journey leads to the legal profession or any other profession outside the arts. It takes discipline and commitment. It teaches you to organize your time, and it also teaches an understanding and appreciation for the talents of other folks, as well."

And that's where the idea for the Brunswick County Courthouse Concert Series came about. "I wanted the courthouse to be more accessible, for the people to feel that this was not just a place to come when legal matters brought them here, and music seemed to be the key. I wanted people to see this building as a positive element in the life of this district." Ola and I discussed the role of music in molding the communities we lived in. A few weeks prior, she and I had judged a local talent contest that featured a diverse group of performers and talents. That had led to our conversation about the courthouse and music: two things in which every citizen shared a common interest.

As Ola talked about her goal of creating a greater feel of accessibility within the courthouse, she explained ways in which music has played (and continues to play) a major role in the history and culture of the country. Military bands play for all kinds of government functions, patriotic songs have become a part of every school chorus repertoire, and, most importantly, Americans have for centuries used music to record the personal and collective triumphs and tragedies that have occurred throughout our history.

There are many who still remember the tragedy of war, but we also remember the music that helped get us through those times. As the battles of war rained terrible horrors upon our country, it was the memory, if not the actual sound, of the popular music of the day that helped so many Americans survive.

That day, Ola and I reminisced about those old songs of our childhood: "The White Cliffs of Dover," "Coming in on a Wing and a Prayer," "Boogie Woogie Bugle Boy," "Don't Sit Under the Apple Tree," and other songs we had listened to with our parents as the World Wars raged in Europe and the Pacific. We remembered the songs that first made us question the world around us—"Blowing in the Wind," "We Shall Overcome," and "If I Had a Hammer"—in the '60s. They didn't have to be protest songs. We wanted to hear what the people of Brunswick county sang at church, at school, and at the beaches. We thought it might be a good idea to find out what this generation's songs are, that way they could voice their identities right here where we lived, where they lived, where we all shared our lives. As Ola saw it, these were the kinds of personal songs that defined our country. Certainly, we needed some encouragement during both good times and bad.

"I hope the performances here in the courthouse will be a personal expression of who we all are," said Ola. And that's why she had chosen to host such an eclectic collection of local performers over the years: Dr. Angela Thompson, James Boston, the Sea Trail Songbirds, high school and elementary school choruses, and professional singers like Dale McPherson and Jeff Krueck. Each month, and always on a Tuesday, the courthouse's rotunda serves as the backdrop for a free, forty-five minute musical performance.

The morning before my conversation with Ola, I had sat in that beautiful rotunda, its winding staircases on each side leading to a landing on the second floor, where four girls comprising a group called "The Voice of Adonai" gave a beautiful gospel performance. The acoustics were wonderful. The girls' voices filled the room and floated down the halls. People came out of offices and stood, many still holding their briefcases, as they awaited the opening of the courtroom. Some of the songs were sung a cappella, the blending of the voices so complete, the harmonies so warm that the listeners, for just a little while, were granted a respite from the legal discord that had brought them there.

As the group sang an up-tempo song, I watched an elderly lady who stood in line, waiting to pass through the building's security gate. She was clutching a walking cane, moving slowly toward the area where the group was performing. As she got closer, she seemed to sense the rhythm of the music. She turned her head to search for the origin of the sound and began to tentatively shuffle her feet in time. I don't know what circumstance had brought her to the courthouse that day, but for just a moment, it took second place to the music.

But it's not just the listeners who were affected by Ola Lewis's dream of making the courthouse more than a place of legal presidings.

Tamara, Shanta, KaRisha, and Sheena, the members of the "Voice of Adonai," said they had "received a blessing." "We just want to sing," one of the young women said. The group of girls, all in their twenties, were pursuing a career in music. They had even sung on America's Got Talent and American Idol but said that "this is special."

"This is home and we appreciate the opportunity to sing in this place."

Dale McPherson had been singing all his life when he was asked to sing at the courthouse. "I saw the reaction of the people," he said. "I've sung for small audiences and large, and I can tell when the people like what they're hearing. I could tell they liked what they heard that day I sang. Ola understands ordinary people and I appreciate that," said Dale. And really, weren't we all just ordinary people?

"I appreciate the opportunity to be a part of bringing the arts to everybody," added Dale, "not just those who can afford to go to a concert. It was a good experience for me as performer and as a resident of Brunswick County."

Ola brought something new and different to the courthouse in Brunswick County. We've all heard that "art is in the eye of the beholder." What is art to one person may not be art to another, but art cannot exist unless it is beheld.

Ola and I had originally met and become friends early on in her role as Resident Superior Court Judge, after she had presided over several family court hearings for children who would eventually become residents of Boys and Girls Homes. Today, Judge Ola Lewis has reached one of the highest levels of the legal profession, has received countless honors and accolades, and has been recognized for her leadership by both her peers and the public she serves. And through music, she continues to bring a sense of unity to her community and an appreciation for the unique talents they each possess.

And she still loves music. Perhaps deep in her heart there still exists that little girl who wants to be a ballerina.

Wayne, George, Loretta, Bobby, and Other Stars

*C*elebrities are often referred to as "stars." Usually, the reference is reserved for those who have become famous or received a lot of acclaim for accomplishments in their respective fields of endeavor: sports stars, movie stars, opera stars, rock stars, TV stars. Over the years, I got to meet a lot of stars, particularly when I was in the television business. Ours were usually brief encounters, short interviews or quick conversations at a reception. Most of them were interesting people. Many were very nice people. Some were jerks, though fame had made them stars regardless. But then there were those stars who fit a more accurate definition; those individuals were bright lights who shined on and guided others to where they wanted to go.

After a short tenure as director of an arts center down in Florida, I came back home to work in the family business in 1980. It was a big change. I went from having shrimp scampi and a glass of wine for lunch at expensive restaurants to balogna sandwiches and Pepsi in the back of the Council and Company store. But I liked it. I'd come back to my roots. I liked working with my family. I liked the routine. I liked the time I had to work with horses. And I liked spending time with my family at home.

I was still singing and emceeing pageants and festivals all over the country at that time, and I was working with a talent agency in Greensboro called Talent Network. They mostly got me television commercials. During the production of one of those commercials, Sandy Long, the account executive from WWAY-TV, (about thirty to forty-five minutes away in Wilmington) happened to be there. She mentioned a project they were doing to "paint a picture of their coverage area." She thought I might be a good host for the project and asked me to meet with the station production manager.

And that's how I met George Allen. He was the production manager at the young station in Wilmington. Like me, he was a native of the Wilmington area who had been with the station since it began in the mid-sixties. He was also one of the happiest and most upbeat people I'd ever met.

In our initial meeting, George asked me what television work I had been doing, and I told him it was mostly commercials.

"Good training," he said. "But not exactly what we're doing here."

I replied, "Well, I can write a little. I've produced a lot of slide shows [way back before taped video and digital presentations were commonplace], taken the photographs, written the scripts, added the music, and done the voice-overs."

George proceeded to tell me more about what they wanted to do with the project and said, "Let me see what you can come up with."

I went back home, sat down in my dining room, and wrote a script along with video instructions for a thirty-minute documentary about Robeson County. I took it back to George the next day. He was surprised at how quickly I had written the story and hired me that day. Over the course of several months, we went on to do a similar presentation of each of the counties in the coverage area.

I would go into the studio with George as he edited the stories, and I learned a lot about the technical production of television programs. During one of those sessions, Sandy Long, the sales rep who had originally introduced me to George, came in. She mentioned that one of the hosts of the morning show on a competing station was leaving to come to WWAY-TV and start a similar morning show. Of course, George knew about this, so I asked why he hadn't told me about it.

"It's a done deal," he answered. "Why don't you go try out for his old job."

With that encouragement, I brazenly and naively walked into the general manager's office at WECT-TV and told them I wanted to apply for the job of co-host on their morning show. The manager, Ernie Whitmeyer, called in Wayne Jackson, the remaining co-host/anchor for the show. I had previously met Wayne and Ernie during the course of my work with WWAY—Wilmington was a small town back then— but this was different. I showed them my resume, such as it was, and talked to them while expounding (and expanding) on my experience at WWAY and Talent Network. After a tour of the station, Ernie said he'd call me the next day.

When Ernie called the next day and told me I had the job, I was ecstatic. After I hung up the phone, I jumped up and down and then ran around the house to find Claudia and tell her the news. I went down to Wilmington that Friday afternoon and signed the contract. I was supposed to go on air Monday morning.

I probably didn't give the local audience the best impression that morning. There was no script, just a format sheet that gave the topics to be discussed, and time lengths for the news, weather, and commercial breaks. At the end of the show, I was worried about my performance, but Wayne assured me I did fine. Wayne Jackson turned out to be a wonderful mentor and friend.

My predecessor had been a fellow named Bob Waters, an expansive man who was a great television personality—and had the ego that often comes with that kind of fame. But he had not been the most reliable when it came to being on time for assignments and, in particular, making it to the studio for an early morning show. So, when a viewer called immediately after the show to talk to Wayne, I was anxious to hear what she said.

"Bill Thompson is a terrible choice to replace Bob," she said. "He is dull, dull, dull. He just didn't have much to say. You and Bob just carried on like it was fun. You need to find somebody else."

She was right. I had not been as ebullient as Bob. I was nervous and afraid to take the lead in the non-scripted conversations that were so much a part of the show. But Wayne's response was a reflection of his professionalism and his willingness to work with a novice. "Well, at least he showed up," he told the lady.

Over the next five years Wayne, and the other veterans in the station, taught me a lot about local television. Wayne had come from a radio background, starting near his hometown not far from Chicago. He had come to North Carolina to work with a station in Rocky Mount, but he wanted to try the ever-expanding medium of television. He had been a sportscaster. Not just a guy who followed sports, he absorbed everything about sports: game rules, players, coaches, statistics, history. And, oh yes, a big Chicago Cubs fan.

When the new television station in Wilmington premiered in 1954, Wayne was hired almost immediately. As with most small-market stations at that time, everybody got involved in every aspect of the operation. Television technology was new. Much of what became television was adapted from radio.

Almost all of the programming was live, original, and local, except for the film that was used for the news and some of the commercials. Wayne did a lot of commercials live. He even hosted a kids' show live.

WMFD, the original call letters for the station, was affiliated with NBC and CBS, and the whole operation was housed on the second floor of the old Murchison Building downtown. Flexibility, adaptation, and innovation were key elements of the broadcasting process. There was no remote equipment at that time, and the cameras in the studio were big and bulky. But Wayne and his technical crew were up to every challenge.

When the big Azalea Festival parade came down the street in front of the Murchison Building that year, they took the big cameras down to the street, ran long lengths of cable out the second-floor windows, and Wayne announced the parade to an appreciative audience who had never before seen that event televised.

Later, when the station changed its call letters to WECT and became an exclusive NBC affiliate, Wayne stayed with the station, eventually moving into new quarters on Shipyard Boulevard. Wayne adapted to the emerging trends in the business as he became a news anchor and, later, the station manager. He was among the few people who provided live news coverage of Hurricane Hazel when it transformed southeastern North Carolina.

Wayne was an "icon" well before that was a common title, and he was already well-established by the time I came to the station. He knew everybody in town, and everybody knew him. I used to tease him about how I'd watched him on a show called "Relax with Jax" when I was just a little boy. When I was in high school, Wayne's visit to our athletic facilities was an exciting event. Being on television every day with Wayne Jackson was a big deal for this boy from Hallsboro.

In the 1980s, programing was still locally-oriented. The Cameron family owned the station and was adamant that it become and remain a big part of the community. And it did. Our show, *Carolina in the Morning*, was a part of the community—a changing community, as large companies moved in and Wilmington's tourist industry boomed. In fact, the show was not originally a part of the news department but rather a separate operation called local programming, which included our show and *The Jim Burns Show*, a mid-morning talk show.

One of my first assignments was to cover the livestock market news each morning. I didn't do that for very long before we determined that hardly anybody cared what hogs and cows were selling for. We continually adapted our program to meet the needs of our audience.

My main responsibility was to go out every day and find stories about the people and places in our area and make those stories interesting. I visited a lot of businesses just to learn more about their industries. Since our coverage area was geographically and culturally diverse, our stories reflected that diversity. One morning after the show, Wayne told me I was to do a profile on the president of a bank that had just merged with another local bank and then meet with a farmer who raised hogs in what was then the emerging operation of raising hogs in confined spaces. When I said I'd better take a change of clothes given the contrasting work places, he said, "Depends on who you see first. The hogs won't mind the suit and tie."

So many of the things I was able to do came about because Wayne had already done that sort of thing. I was still excited to meet celebrities, though Wayne was a little jaded. The Azalea Festival always brought big-time celebrities to town—Barbara Mandrell, Wayne Newton, Bob Hope, Charley Pride, Johnny Mathis, soap opera stars, Miss America (several of them), Johnny Bench, Barbara Eden, Kim Morgan Greene, Burt Reynolds, Joe Namath, Arnold Palmer, Bill Anderson, Dolly Parton, Alan Alda, and more. I usually interviewed them when they visited the station, but sometimes I'd meet them elsewhere while they were in town. But Wayne liked doing the political interviews. During an election, we would have many of the candidates either come on the show or we would go to Raleigh and talk to them. Local representatives, state senators and representatives, mayors, and governors were frequent guests.

Wayne and I were our own producers, which gave us a lot of freedom in determining what we put on the air. As long as we didn't violate any FCC regulations, we had free rein to do whatever stories we wanted. In 1984, we decided we would have every candidate for governor of North Carolina come on the show. One of those candidates was Glenn Miller, leader of the Carolina Knights of the Ku Klux Klan, who was seeking the Democratic nomination. We had made a big deal out of the fact that we were going to let our audience meet everybody running for the governor's office, but we had not invited Mr. Miller. So, Miller called Wayne one day and said he thought he should be on the show. Wayne relented and Miller showed up at the studio one morning at about five o'clock, accompanied by four armed bodyguards.

One of the station's housekeepers was a wonderful black lady named Loretta Smith. She usually began her work about the time we went on the air each morning. Many of those mornings, Loretta would fix breakfast for Wayne and me in the employee lounge and also let those guests who were to be on the show in through the back door of the news room. That morning, we had not told Loretta who our next guest was, only that his name was Glenn Miller.

When Miller and his entourage arrived, Loretta let them in. They marched by her without saying a word. Loretta was one of those people who was just naturally friendly. As the group walked by her, she felt the need to welcome them to the station. She said, "Mr. Miller, I sure do enjoy your music. Y'all going to play some this morning?"

Fortunately, she didn't get a reply. After they had gone into the studio, I asked Loretta if she knew who he was. She said, "Y'all said he was Glenn Miller and I got a bunch of Glenn Miller records." After I told her who he really was, she said, "I bet he can't dance either."

Most of my stories were feature stories—what some journalists call "fluff pieces." They could be longer than straight news pieces and could involve as much creativity as I could muster: natural sound, music and even poetry. That took a lot of editing time, but I enjoyed the process. I edited most of my own pieces, although a photographer shot the raw video. Two people, Bobby Jordan and Bobby Long, taught me how to edit. Bobby Jordan was head of production, and he explained that the more I learned to do by myself, the more job security I would have. My goal was to produce stories to match those Charles Kuralt put on his *On the Road* series and *CBS Sunday Morning*.

Apart from teaching me how to conduct on-air interviews, Wayne taught me a lot about local journalism. There have always been members of the print news profession who have a somewhat condescending view of broadcast journalism. To them, television news is more entertainment than information. In more recent years, that opinion might have even more support than it did when I was gathering and reporting news on the air. But for any journalist, it is a real challenge to gather all the facts of a story and write it concisely enough to fit into a ninety-second video.

One key element Wayne always stressed in putting any story together was, "let the pictures tell the story as much a possible." While we had a lot of leeway in choosing what we ran as feature stories on the morning show, reporting the news was just as important at six o'clock in the morning as it was at six o'clock in the evening.

Since we were not a part of the news department, we had to rely on our own sources. Our primary source was the wire service. My first job every morning was to check the teletype machines and see if there was any news that had happened since the eleven o'clock news the night before, particularly if it was local or had a local impact. If there was something we could use that morning, I tore off the yellow pages and put them in the pile to be read during the news segments (literally) "rip and read." We didn't have teleprompters on the morning show, because we didn't have time to put together the long sheet of copy that would need to be fed into the machine. By far our biggest source of "new news" was the morning edition of the *Star News,* our local newspaper. Condensing and re-writing a newspaper story to fit a tight time slot and still tell the most important parts was always a challenge, particularly when we had no video to go with it. Other than that, we used whatever copy was left that had been used at eleven and combined it with any calls we'd received ourselves that morning, including news releases.

The show was very popular. When the other station across town started their own morning show, we almost always beat them in the ratings. When they would occasionally beat us, I would question the authenticity of the results. Wayne once told me something that applied not only to ratings, but to everything in life: "If you believe it when it's in your favor, you have to believe it when it's against you."

When I left WECT in 1987, I didn't leave my friends behind. In fact, during the next several years as I worked to promote Boys Home, I relied on my friends at the station to help me get the word out and, often, to raise funds more directly.

In 1995, Boys Homes had constructed a new covered arena on the farm. One of the most popular events held there was a rodeo. At one point I decided to see if we could expand that event to include television. So, I went to see George at WWAY and told him what I wanted to do. He asked, "You want to do a live broadcast of a rodeo? Do you know how complicated and expensive that would be?"

I told him I didn't know, and that's why I had come to him. After considerable discussion, we determined that such a broadcast was not possible. But we decided we could tape the rodeo and broadcast it later. Video tape had been brand new technology when I first met George. By the time we talked about the rodeo, it had become everyday stuff.

Tim Horton, who was the production manager at the time, and I decided I would share the announcing duties with Roger Harris, the contractor for the rodeo and a fantastic announcer. Before the rodeo began, Roger and I would ride into the arena on horseback, welcome everybody to the show, then exit. Tim and his crew would tape the entire rodeo, then, sometime in the next week or so, Roger and I would go to the studio in Wilmington, sit in a darkened editing booth, and narrate a one-hour edited version of the rodeo. It was a lot more complicated than live TV, but it was worth it. We were able to sell commercial time during the broadcast too, thus gaining additional revenue for Boys and Girls Homes as well as for the station. The project went well, and we continued to do the televised shows until Roger was tragically killed in an accident on his farm.

⌒

Wayne, Bobby, Loretta, George, and so many others who were colleagues during those television days remained friends. The years I spent with them were some of the happiest in my life, and working as a morning show host was the best job I ever had. The pay was terrible, but the experiences and the people I met were priceless.

The Devil's Trail Ride and Other TV Interviews

robably one of the biggest reasons I liked doing the morning show on WECT was the flexibility I had in producing the stories to be presented each morning. Their more recent programming in years since I left has been less flexible. Since Wayne Jackson and I were our own producers, it was up to us to decide the type of story we would cover, including the length of the piece. Often, we would respond to calls from viewers who had suggestions or, more often, we would just be curious about something and would seek out that person or event. Such was the case with Ray Stewart of Godwin, North Carolina.

I had met Ray when I was working with H.J. White in the horse and magazine business. Ray was a construction contractor who loved horses. H.J. and I had contracted with him to provide the dirt footing for the first rodeo staged in the then new Cumberland County Arena in Fayetteville. Ray had a farm and horse training facility near Godwin close to the upper Cape Fear River. He and his sons trained trail horses using the woods, fields, and river.

When we were working on the rodeo, Ray had told me about his horses and how he trained them. He said, "When we get a horse we think is about as good as we going to get him on trails, we take him on a ride down by the river. If he does well, we consider him graduated from trail school. We invite other folks to go with us 'cause it's a lot of fun. You oughta come some time."

That invitation had come several years before I began working at the television station, but I remembered it when a mutual friend told me he was going on the "Devil's Trail Ride." Of course, the name intrigued me, and when I asked more about it, I realized it was the event Ray had told me about. I thought it would be a great story for the morning show if I took a photographer along on the ride.

I called Ray, and he said, "Come on. You'll like it. But you better have a camera man who can ride pretty good." Fortunately, Warren Bess, the photographer assigned to our show, could ride. He didn't claim to be a great horseman, but he was excited about doing the story.

The morning of the ride, Warren and I arrived early at Ray's barn. He met us and took us inside, where he picked out a couple of horses he said were well-trained and had been on the ride many times. Warren had responsibility for the bulky video equipment. We didn't have modern compact digital equipment. Instead, we had a big, bulky shoulder camera and a separate, equally heavy and clumsy cassette recorder that was attached to the camera by a cord. Both units ran on batteries.

We had considered using a pack-horse arrangement for the equipment, but Warren decided he needed the video equipment on the same horse he was riding. So, Ray used a creative hitch and secured the recorder behind Warren's saddle. Then, Warren had to hold the camera in front of him with one hand and hold the horse's reins with the other.

By the time we got everything put together, several other folks had joined us. All of them were seasoned trail riders, including Jerry, a soldier stationed at Fort Bragg. Jerry said he had heard about the "Devil's Trail Ride" and was looking forward to the challenge. He had brought along his own horse that he said was "tough enough to look the devil in the eye and not even blink."

We were an eclectic safari: ten horses of different colors and ten riders—some of us wearing leather chaps to protect our legs from the brush, some wearing cowboy hats, and some wearing baseball caps—as our line silently wound through the green foliage. Occasionally, Warren would break from the line and go ahead or to the side to get a shot of the troop.

We didn't talk much.

We concentrated on where our horses went and where they stepped. To say the trail was a challenge would be a grave understatement. It ran through a variety of terrains, from flat, open meadows to thick brush, to steep hills. When going down some of those hills, the horses' rumps would slide in the deep trenches that had been created by previous challengers.

The plan was to cross the Cape Fear River at a narrow point, then rest and eat lunch before heading back. It was a very warm day, and we took frequent rest stops to let the horses—and the riders—cool off a little. When we got to the river, Ray gave instructions on how to ford it. This section was a shallow crossing that would not require the horses to swim, but the water would probably be chest high on our mounts. He told us not to guide the horses. "Give 'em their head. They know how to get across. You just hold on."

Ray started the group across. The river current was slow, but the water was cold. The horses and riders shivered as the water wrapped around us, washing away the sweat of a sweltering Carolina summer. Warren had dismounted and was taping the scene from the river bank. At some point, Warren's horse decided to cross the river with the others. The horse calmly walked into the water with the recorder still attached to the camera that sat on Warren's shoulder. Warren couldn't hold on to the camera and the horse, so he quickly detached the cord between the camera and the recorder. Just as Ray had said, the horse knew how to cross the river, even without a rider. Ray's son, Rocky, reached out and caught the reins of Warren's horse as he came up beside the animal and brought him back to the riverbank. Warren calmly reattached the cord and continued taping.

On the way back, we were sliding down the side of a hill in a rut created by the trail's overuse. Suddenly, Jerry's horse slid into the back of Warren's, causing both horses and riders to crash to the ground. Neither horses nor riders were hurt, so both men remounted and we then continued back to the barn.

As we were unsaddling, I heard Jerry say to Ray, "I believe I'd rather go back and fight the Viet Cong with a switch than try that again." That was probably an over-statement, but nonetheless, the horse that could "meet the devil and not blink," had blinked.

On the way back to the station, Warren and I discussed how we wanted to edit the story. We were pleased with our effort. It wasn't until we got back to the station and Warren was unloading the tapes from the recorder that we noticed the mud on the recorder case. Apparently, probably in the collision and slide down the hill, the red clay of the Cape Fear riverbank had attached itself to the recorder. None of the tapes were damaged, but some of the mud had made its way into the machine itself.

Neither one of us wanted to face the wrath of the engineer who would have to try to salvage the expensive piece of equipment, so Warren just took the damaged goods to the engineering room and left them without a word. Bill Elks was the chief engineer who had been at the station almost from its inception. He was very good at his job. He also had little patience with non-technical reporters like me.

The next morning when I came in, there was a note on my desk from Bill that said in big letters, "SEE ME." After that morning's show, I reluctantly went looking for Bill Elks, expecting to be severely chastised. Fortunately, Warren was already in the engineering room talking to Bill, and Bill was smiling. As it turned out, Warren's explanation was so "unique" (Bill's words) that we both escaped chastisement.

Mrs. St. George

In the fall of 1983, a viewer's suggestion for a story resulted in one of the funniest interviews I ever did for WECT. The viewer said there was a lady down in Southport who was really making a name for herself as a potter. This lady's original creations were very popular, and she had gained recognition from prominent art critics from New York and Boston, as well winning a lot of regional awards.

The lady's name was Laura St. George. When I called Mrs. St. George, she seemed genuinely surprised we wanted to do a story about her, but she agreed to meet us at the senior citizen center there in Southport where she had her studio.

In order to do a proper interview, we needed to set up some extra lighting in addition to providing microphones for Mrs. St. George and me. Also, we decided to use two cameras, so there was a small group of us traveling to Southport.

Mrs. St. George had some of her work displayed at the center, and we asked if she could set up her potter's wheel and work on a piece while we did the interview. After she got everything set up, I sat down across from her as we began the interview. She had a piece of clay on the wheel and a small container of water beside her. As we talked, she turned the potter's wheel by using a foot pedal. She added water occasionally to the clay, molding it into whatever she had in mind.

As in most interviews, we wanted to get enough taped footage to edit the piece down to the appropriate length, so I asked her several questions as she worked. As she answered the questions, she would sometimes stop the wheel, push the clay back into the amorphous shape she had started with, then continue working.

After we had been talking for several minutes, I asked, "Now, Mrs. St. George, what is this piece you are making here?"

She stopped the wheel and said with a little frustration in her voice, "Well, it started out to be a bowl, but I've been talking to you so long I don't know what in the hell it is!" I left her response in the edited version.

Not too long after our interview, Mrs. St. George passed away and her son, Daniel, brought me a little trivet she had made for me. I still have it. I keep it as a kind of memorial to a talented—and patient—lady.

Venus and the Beauty Queens

When you grow up in a small Southern town and want to be a performer, your path toward that goal might take an unusual route, particularly if you are a man.

I followed the usual course of school and church, singing in glee club and in several different choirs, but it wasn't until I was married and supporting a family that I found a way to sing for a secular audience beyond the private parties for which my sister and I had sung as college students.

My work with Boys and Girls Homes had put me in touch with a lot of civic clubs, including the Jaycees. That was an organization of young men who were, just as the name implied, the Junior Chamber of Commerce members who promoted their communities. The North Carolina Jaycees were sponsors of the Miss North Carolina Scholarship Pageant, a yearly event that selected one young lady to represent the state at various functions and then compete for the Miss America title. Local Jaycee chapters sponsored pageants that would select a young lady to promote their respective community and compete for the Miss North Carolina title. I became a member of the Lake Waccamaw Jaycees, who were co-sponsors with the other Jaycee chapters in the Miss Columbus County Pageant.

One year in the early '70s, Patsy Johnson, Miss North Carolina 1969, was scheduled to be the emcee for the county pageant. For whatever reason, she called on the Friday before the Saturday night pageant to say she would be unable to appear. In the tradition of old Hollywood movies, I was called in to substitute for her. As a result of the appearance, some of the judges for that pageant asked me to be the emcee for their local pageant—and it went on from there.

Over the years, I emceed and entertained for hundreds of Miss America preliminary pageants and festival pageants across the South. And, Lord knows, the South is famous for pageantry. I once ventured to say that every Southern girl I knew had been, was, or would be in some kind of beauty pageant.

I once wrote a short story about a girl in a local pageant and wrote it in the first person from the perspective of the girl. Someone asked me why I felt qualified to write from the contestant's perspective. I told them I had known hundreds of beautiful, talented, smart pageant girls. I also had raised one and married two.

I was qualified.

Pageants also allowed me to meet some of the finest people in the world. Despite my generally cynical attitude, I found that most of the people who promoted, produced, and judged pageants did so because they really believed the contestants were benefiting from being in the competition. Maybe all of them didn't think that way, but most did. I did, or else I would not have continued to be a part of so many for so long.

Pageants gave small-town girls a reason to wear beautiful formal clothes as well as a chance to display and hone their talents. If they won, they got to travel to places they would have never visited and meet people they would have never encountered otherwise.

One of the most remarkable pageant people I met was Venus Wallace. Venus was first of all a newspaperwoman. In a small-town newspaper, the reporter, publisher, columnist, and printer are sometimes all the same person. Venus was each of those things. She died around the time I began writing this book. Her passing brought back a lot of memories for me, including a visit I made just a few years ago. She was officially retired, but she still had that "nose for news" that comes from years in the business. And she had definite opinions about it all. During my visit, we talked about politics (she was against the general practice of it), the economy ("what's left of it"), and people in the news ("most celebrities are tacky people").

Nobody would have suspected Venus was a pageant advocate. She never adopted a glamourous persona. When I would stop in the newspaper office for a visit, I would usually find Venus clad in the requisite T-shirt and jeans, cigarette smoke drifting across piles of photos and papers like incense offered to the God of the Fourth Estate. She did dress up a little bit for the pageants themselves, but Venus was, first and foremost, a newspaperwoman.

She was just as interested in the outcome of the high school football game as she was in knowing the winner of a pageant. She was tough. Again, not exactly the kind of woman you'd expect to be a champion of beauty pageants. But Venus was unconventional.

I first met Venus back in the early '70s when I was emceeing a lot of pageants and festivals around the state. Venus was there for most of them, taking photographs for *The Denton Record*, the local newspaper she ran with her husband, Ed. They sold the paper in 1995 and then Ed passed away in 2002. They had met when both were students at Catawba College. Ed was originally from New Jersey, and Venus was as Southern as you could get. They both appreciated all the things that made up a small Southern town and loved being a part of it, warts and all. We shared a time and place unique in America and friends just as unique.

Those folks we used to know were "pageant folks"—contestants, judges, performers—people all across the state who constituted an element of North Carolina culture that has diminished in the past years. There were a lot of old Jaycees like me: Gary Sherrill, McNeil Chestnut, Steve Googe, Wayne Hicks, and David Ward, who became a big part of the Miss North Carolina program and chose to stay involved after they passed the age of "Jayceeism" (thirty-five years old at that time). Their participation provided a thread of continuity, experience, and expertise to the state organization and lasting friendships for me.

So, how did a newspaperwoman like Venus discover and develop an interest in beauty pageants?

Back in our day, there was a pageant, either a Miss North Carolina preliminary or a festival pageant, in almost every city, town, and hamlet. On my visit with Venus that afternoon several years ago, she reminded me that she and Ed had become involved in pageants because Ed was a member of the Denton Lions Club, which sponsored the Miss Denton Pageant. As a devoted partner to her husband, Venus directed that pageant and, as newspaper people, they looked for ways to promote the town through the pageant.

Eventually, *The Denton Record* began to run a page every week about where Miss Denton had been. That turned out to be just about everywhere in North Carolina. Both the pageant and Denton benefited from the exposure. Everybody who sponsored a pageant subscribed to *The Denton Record* so they could see the pictures of their respective queens posing with Miss Denton. For no additional cost to the paper, all those folks had begun to learn about and love the little town in the middle of the state.

The promotional effort was a family affair. "Suzi and Theresa [her teenaged daughters] were not real happy about going to all those pageants," Venus remembered. "They would distribute copies of the paper to all the folks who attended the pageants. That was not very glamourous compared to being a part of the elaborate stage productions that were put on back then. But it was an effective way to get people to read about Denton."

As we began to reminisce about those pageants, I remembered some of the participants and wondered where they were. Venus knew, of course. Susan Lawrence Googe, for instance, became like family and had remained in touch with Venus. Susan had been Miss North Carolina in 1975. "She's just as pretty now as she was when she was Miss North Carolina," Venus said. Susan married Steve Googe who was, at the time of our conversation, the director of economic development in Davidson

County, and they had two grown sons. Venus was there for all of Susan's big moments—Miss Thomasville to Miss North Carolina to Susan and Steve's wedding.

"Other than the pageant, the only time I saw her in a dress was at my wedding," Susan said of Venus. "There was usually a reception following a pageant, but she always wanted a late-night meal at Waffle House."

That unconventional attitude carried over into Venus's view of pageants in general. "Back then, pageants were serious events," Venus said. "I still believe that girls should be ladies. [The contestants] had the responsibility of representing their communities. It involved a lot of time and commitment. At the same time, I wanted them to be themselves too, not fit into some cookie-cutter cliché of a beauty queen." Venus admired girls with independent spirits much like her own. "I never cared much for 'system' pageants where very young girls entered more for their mama than because they wanted to."

Steve Googe, Susan's husband, reminded me that *The Denton Record* became a kind of unofficial newsletter for the Miss North Carolina Pageant. Googe was in charge of communicating with all the local pageants. Because everybody read the Denton paper, with Ed and Venus's help, the pageant organization could use the paper to keep up to date with all the pageants across North Carolina. Ed and Venus would print the pageant results and a photo of the winner, and always at their own expense.

She and Ed attended town council meetings and were involved in every community activity that came along. "Newspapering is a full-time business," Venus told me. "And covering town news kept us busy. Many times, we'd cover three or four pageants a weekend, as well as the high school ball games. We'd have someone phone in the results of the pageant, but most of the time, we tried to get there personally."

Making it to all of those events would have been a tough task under any circumstance. But, you see, Venus never learned to drive a car. She relied on others, including judge and emcee, Janet Hogan, to give her a ride.

"It was hectic sometimes," Venus said. "Sometimes we didn't know exactly where we were going or how to get there, but Janet would come from Norman [Janet's hometown in Richmond County], pick me up in Denton, and we'd go to Asheville or Morehead City or any of the other hundred towns in the state for the weekend. We had a great time and never had a wreck."

For me, visiting with Venus was more than just nostalgic conversation. I'm only one of many who cherished her friendship and appreciated all she did for the state and her community. I'm personally grateful for the fact that *The Denton Record* was one of the first newspapers to carry my column.

After she retired, Venus quit smoking, spent time working on crossword puzzles (in ink), and "doing as little as possible" while watching old movies, admiring the achievements of her children and grandchildren, and talking with visitors.

She never wore a tiara on her head or a satin sash across her shoulder; she never waved a scepter; but Venus was still a queen. Tiaras and typewriters, lipstick and printer's ink, the musical stage productions and town council meetings were all a part of her realm. For Venus, it was all in a day's work and no conflict at all.

Bess Truman and Me

When you're twelve years old, events either make a big impression on your memory or you don't remember them at all. Meeting and talking with a former president of the United States and his wife certainly made an impression on me, but some of the details have faded after sixty-three years.

꩜

When I was in the eighth grade, I had my first introduction to North Carolina history. I immediately seized on the subject and pursued that interest for the rest of my life. One of my first efforts in learning where I fit into that history was the research I did for a paper about the origin of my home town of Hallsboro.

In 1955, the North Carolina Literary and Historical Society sponsored a contest for eighth-grade students in which the students would write a history of their home towns. The winner would have his paper published by the society and be recognized at the annual meeting in Raleigh. My eighth-grade teacher was Mr. George Smith. He encouraged me to enter the contest and write about Hallsboro, so I did. In all honesty, that encouragement consisted of giving me the address to where the paper was to be sent. Other than that, I was pretty much on my own and was the only student at our school to participate.

There was not a lot of written history at that time about Hallsboro. It was a small rural community, not even incorporated. (It had been incorporated at one time, but the charter was allowed to expire for reasons probably having to do with the benefit—or lack thereof—of paying municipal taxes.) The community was fairly prosperous as far as small towns went. Hallsboro was home to three or four very active lumber mills supported by a force of independent and contracted loggers, three general stores, a fish market, two barber shops (one white, one black), two auto repair shops (one white, one black), a soda shop, a laundry/dry cleaners, a movie theater, a plethora of churches, and, of course, the two schools (one white, one black). The area around the town was populated by farmers. And, of course, there was the artery that supported it all: a railroad.

Because of the lack of specific written records of the town's development, I had to rely on personal recollections of the current inhabitants. I interviewed those people, made copious notes on long, yellow legal pads, and proceeded to write it all out in pencil. One person I interviewed was Mrs. Margaret Merritt, the widow of one of the early sawmill superintendents. She lived in the biggest house in Hallsboro and was a social Brahmin, always serving as a leader in the community. She was a very prim and proper lady. She served tea on the occasion of our interview, and I didn't know what to do. So, she taught me proper tea etiquette, instruction that helped me on later occasions.

My Aunt Hilda Council was an English teacher at the local high school. She reviewed what I wrote, made corrections and suggestions, typed it for me, and helped me package the paper to send to Raleigh.

My Grandmother Council was also a major resource for me in writing the paper. She read my paper before I sent it in and gave her approval, a Royal Acknowledgement from the modest and reticent Queen of Hallsboro.

I don't think Mr. Smith ever saw it.

A lot of time passed before I heard from the society. At last, I got a letter from Mr. Christopher Crittenden, secretary of the society, informing me that my story had been selected as the winner, and I was to come to the annual meeting in Raleigh that December to receive my award. I remember getting the letter; that was probably one of the happiest moments of my life. I had worked hard and been recognized for it. No one else I knew had won anything like that. I showed the letter to my family, and they were all ecstatic. I asked Aunt Hilda if she would go with me to Raleigh, but she declined, pointing out that only three people could make the trip. I don't know if I even told Mr. Smith about it, and he never asked.

The meeting was held in the old Sir Walter Raleigh Hotel in Raleigh, an impressive building that was the unofficial center of state politics at that time. I remember it was cold as we walked down Fayetteville street to the hotel. We found our way to the meeting area, presented our letter to a lady sitting at a desk outside the meeting room, and went and sat in the very back row. I sat between Mama and Daddy, which didn't give me a very good view of the speaker's platform. But as we sat there in contemplation of what was to come, a gentleman approached us and asked if I was William Thompson. After I told him I was William Thompson, he asked me to follow him. We went down to the first row of chairs in the room, and the man said, "William, I would like to introduce you to Mrs. Bess Truman. She is the wife of President Truman."

It took me a second to realize he was talking about the former president of the United States, Mr. Harry S. Truman. I had seen Mrs. Truman's picture in the newspaper, but she didn't look like that in person. She looked like my grandmothers, both of them. She reached out and shook my hand and asked, "How do you do, William?"

To tell you the truth, I don't know what I answered. I just shook her hand and looked at her in awe. I was meeting the former First Lady of the United States of America! Me: a twelve-year-old boy from a dot on the map called Hallsboro. Then she asked me to sit beside her there in the front row. I did. After I sat down, she said some other things to me, which I don't remember, then she turned and talked to other people. Once in a while, she would turn to me and introduce me to some of those people, but I didn't know them then nor now.

It wasn't long after I joined Mrs. Truman that Mr. Crittenden introduced Mr. Truman. As the former president walked out, I stood up with everyone else in the place and applauded, then sat back down, even more awed by the occasion than I had been before. I don't recall much of what Mr. Truman spoke about, but I believe it had something to do with Civil War history. The only specific thing I remember was his reference to a Union general named Butler who supposedly stole all of the silverware in the city when he took New Orleans. According to Mr. Truman, that is how he got the nickname "Spoon" Butler. I was just twelve years old; that kind of thing interested me.

Sometime after Mr. Truman's speech, I received my award and was officially designated a "Young Historian." Mr. Crittenden presented me with the award, and Mr. Truman shook my hand and congratulated me.

The only other thing I remember from that occasion was the reception after the meeting. It was held right outside the meeting room, and Mrs. Truman asked if I thought my parents would like to join us for the reception. I said yes, and she asked where they were seated. I pointed them out to her at the back of the room. Then she took my hand and walked with me back to where Mama and Daddy were seated. She shook hands with them and asked them to join us in the lobby. I don't know if I have ever been so impressed with anybody since that time. In the course of my life, I have met some famous people but never one as humble and warm as Bess Truman. The former First Lady of the United States spoke with us as if we had been friends forever. She asked about Hallsboro and our family. This lady who had hosted state dinners at the White House was also the lady from Independence, Missouri, who had hosted her husband's friends for poker games in her kitchen. This lady in the simple wool coat had attended both historic ceremonies in European capitals and her daughter's music recitals in small auditoriums. She had chefs prepare her meals in the White House but cooked for her husband and her mother-in-law in her small kitchen in Independence. And when "the weight of the world" had fallen on her husband, she helped him lift it by encouraging him to return to 219

North Delaware Street in Independence, a respite from the pressure of the White House.

Mrs. Truman never sought the spotlight like her predecessor, Eleanor Roosevelt. She was content to stay in the background. But to that small boy that night in Raleigh, meeting her was like meeting a queen, a queen of a democratic country, her crown a small straw hat pinned to her gray hair. She was the queen of the United States of America just like my grandmother was the Queen of Hallsboro, North Carolina. Both very honorable positions.

Mr. Charlie Harrington: Horseman

*T*he cold wind blew across the pasture, stirred the broom straw, and created a brown wave that undulated down to the swamp. Mr. Charlie Harrington seemed to hardly notice the cold as he followed me toward the herd of mares that had settled out of the wind in a clump of sweetgum trees. At ninety-three years old, his eyesight had deteriorated considerably and his step was a little slower. But he was determined to see the newest foal that had been born that morning.

He didn't know how many foals had begun their lives on Honey Hill Farm, but he knew that each was different in some way. When we reached the herd, I saw a dark bay mare and her foal resting under one of the trees. Mr. Harrington held on to my arm as we approached the pair. The mare stood up and nickered as we approached. I was afraid she was going to run off with her foal, but Mr. Harrington spoke softly, "Whoa, girl. It's just me; we just want to see your baby."

The mare lowered her head and stood facing us as Mr. Harrington cautiously reached out to her. He placed his hand on the mare's neck, rubbing it and running his fingers through her tangled mane. He continued to talk softly as he ran his hand down her flanks, down past her hocks, and to her back feet where the newborn foal lay. Slowly, still holding on to my arm, the old man knelt beside the baby, talking softly.

"It's still a little wet," Mr. Harrington noted as he ran his hand over the newborn foal. "A little filly," he said, announcing that the new foal was a girl.

With some effort, the old man pulled himself back up and then we started back toward the barn. "She'll be a good one. Her mama and her daddy were good cutting horses, knew how to work cattle." Mr. Harrington knew the bloodlines of every horse on Honey Hill Farm. "Call Dr. Burns and get him down here and make sure they're both alright," he instructed. I had agreed to work with Mr. Harrington's horses in exchange for boarding mine.

"This weather's gonna be tough on 'em," I said.

"They'll be fine," he said. "Horses ought to be born outside. Not natural for them to be born inside. Put them inside with all the dust and mold and other stuff, and they'll have less chance of making it."

As always, Mr. Harrington was right. He knew horses. He had raised horses for many years. He told me once that when he first started raising horses, there had been only a few automobiles in Wilmington. Horses were necessities.

Mr. Harrington was a wealthy man in many ways. His business, Hyman Supply Company, was a very successful building and plumbing supply business he had purchased from the Hyman family. The North Carolina Lumber Company had been one of his customers, and when they sold out and moved from the area, Honey Hill Farm had been transferred to Mr. Harrington to help satisfy their debt to Hyman Supply.

He had originally bred and raised standardbred trotting horses on the farm at Honey Hill. In fact, one of the old sulkies was still upstairs in the hayloft. He had shown them at state fairs and races all over the east coast. But sometime in the late 1950s, he had started breeding registered American Quarter Horses. Quarter Horses are primarily stock horses used to work cattle. They seemed to fit in with the cattle program at the farm. Previously, he had bred, raised, and shown Herefords, but he switched to Black Angus as that breed had become more popular in the show ring.

For many years, Art Pitzer managed the farm, but about the time Mr. Harrington changed to a Quarter Horse operation, Art became the director of the North Carolina State Fair. So, Mr. Harrington brought Junior Stewart to the farm to manage the operation. Art and Junior were different in many ways. Art was college educated with a strong background in agricultural management and animal husbandry. Junior was a cowboy with years of practical experience in working stock horses and cattle. Each was very good at his job and singularly qualified for the program at Honey Hill. I didn't know Art Pitzer very well, but I knew Junior. Mr. Harrington had told me once that they were both good horsemen. He said, "All cowboys aren't horsemen and all horsemen aren't cowboys. You're lucky if you can match 'em up to whatever you want to do with your horses." Mr. Harrington was able to do that. Art was more the "stockman" and Junior was more of a "cowboy," but both remained good at the job as the operation changed its focus.

Honey Hill Farm was just a few miles from Hallsboro, and I used to go down there often to visit with Junior. (He and his family lived in an old house on the farm. This was the same house in which my mother's family had previously lived, when my Grandfather Council was in charge of the commissary for the North Carolina Lumber Company.) In addition to pasture and hay fields, Honey Hill Farm also consisted of about another 500 acres of field crops and forest land.

I would sometimes go with Junior to bring the cattle in to be used in training the cutting horses on the farm. Junior would put me on a untrained horse that needed some work. He said I could learn more from a green horse than I could from a more seasoned horse. That may be true, but I think Junior just enjoyed seeing me get thrown by those young horses. Though I did learn a lot.

In 1980, when I came back from Florida and went to work with my family in the oil distributorship, one of the first things I did was go down to visit with Junior and Mr. Harrington. To my surprise and disappointment, I found that Junior had moved on to another job, one that did not involve horses. I remembered that Junior's wife had always wanted him to find a job that paid better. But Junior loved working at Honey Hill. He loved horses and he loved the freedom Mr. Harrington gave him in managing the horse and cattle operation.

I knew Mr. Harrington came down to the farm every Monday morning. So, one morning I went down there to meet him and ask about the possibility of selling a mare he had. My daughter, like almost every little girl, had decided she wanted a horse, and I was going to buy one for her Christmas present. After a long visit and reminiscing, I bought the horse. Part of the deal was I could keep the horse there on the farm as long as I provided all the feed and other care.

A short time after I bought the mare, Mr. Harrington mentioned he had about twenty-five "long yearlings" (horses more than a year and a half old but not yet two), colts and fillies, that needed handling so that they would be gentle enough to have their feet trimmed, cleaned up, and be taken to a sale. Junior had been gone about a year, and Mr. Harrington had not found a replacement. Consequently those young horses had not even been broken to lead much less become gentle enough to handle. Whatever vaccinations they received had to be given by constraining them in a chute. The outcome of the discussion was that I would undertake the challenge of getting those horses ready to sell. My pay would be free board for my horses (by then I had acquired another horse for myself) and the first pick of the next year's foal crop.

I had often heard that experience was the best teacher. I had ridden horses since I was a little boy—both at my grandmother's in Chadbourn and on trails with my cousin's horse in the Elbow section of Hallsboro— and I had participated in rodeo while I was in college. But I didn't have a lot of experience in working with colts, so my arrangement with Mr. Harrington was educational.

I learned a lot about horses in the next few months. Every break I got from working at the family business, I spent at Honey Hill. Every Monday morning, Mr. Harrington would be at the farm. His son, Charlie Jr., would drive him from Wilmington. I would bring all the horses up to the barn, run them into a big pen on the inside, and Mr. Harrington would walk among them. Some had made more progress than others, and I was always worried they might kick, paw, or bite Mr. Harrington as he touched them, because his failing eyesight required him to evaluate each by touch alone.

One morning, I rode my horse down into the pasture to run the yearlings up to the barn. I had left the gate to the indoor pen open. Unbeknownst to me, Mr. Harrington had gone into the pen. By the time I saw him, the herd was headed at a gallop toward the barn. I shouted at Mr. Harrington, and his son shouted at him too, but to no avail. The old man remained in the middle of the pen. The horses rushed from the pasture and into the barn, not stopping until they had encircled him. Although they pushed each other around, the horses never even brushed Mr. Harrington.

When I got to the barn, Charlie Jr. was chastising his father for being so careless. "I was never in any danger," Mr. Harrington said. "These horses know me. They would never hurt me." Who could argue with that? We had just seen a maelstrom of horses envelope a blind man without causing him any injury.

I'd learned over time that Mr. Harrington's wealth extended beyond his financial success. Not many men got to feel the connection to horses that Mr. Harrington had. He understood the animals and there seemed to be an intangible connection between him and the horses he cared so much about. Not everybody got so much satisfaction from that connection.

Even as his health continued to deteriorate, he would have Charlie Jr. drive him to the farm. Sometimes Mr. Harrington would just sit on the office porch and look out over the pastures toward the horses he couldn't see. "I feel 'em," he told me once. "I can see 'em in my mind."

Mr. Harrington lived to be a hundred years old. His family had a birthday celebration for him at his home in Wilmington. I missed the party, but I went down there the day after to see him. He was upstairs in his bedroom at the big house in Forrest Hills. When I got up there, I saw he was hooked up to a bunch of machines, wires, and tubes running everywhere.

He had completely lost his sight by then, but when he heard me, he said, "Hey, Bill. Tell me about the horses."

So, I did.

As I talked about the horses, the years fell away. The old man in the bed became young again, riding out on the green pastures to check on his horses, the foals nursing from mares as they grazed the tall grass.

Then, trying to find something positive about his becoming a centenarian, I asked, "Well, Mr. Harrington, how does it feel to be a big one hundred years old?"

He answered, "Well, I'll tell you, Bill. It's not what it's cracked up to be. Let's talk about the horses."

The filly that was born that cold morning when we'd walked out into the pasture years before had been my pay for getting all those unruly colts and fillies ready to sell. I named her Mayflower. The lady who lived on the farm and helped feed the horses said that when she'd first seen the foal, all she could see was one white foot in the high grass. It reminded her of a mayflower. The filly's registered name was Hill's Mayflower no. 2528951. For the next thirty years, Mayflower and I shared our lives.

I can only imagine what Mr. Harrington felt as he shared his life with so many Mayflowers.

The Quest

It may sound too sentimental, but horses have probably had as much influence on my life as any human. I've bred and raised them, trained them, taken them in the show ring and on trail rides, and worked cattle with them. In looking back on my life, I have searched for those defining moments that tell me about the things I value most. Every once in a while, one of those defining moments comes along and you don't realize its significance until it's gone.

Up until a few years ago, I kept some horses in a pasture next to my house. One of those horses was Mayflower. During the almost thirty years we were together, she had been a constant through job changes, births, deaths, marriages, divorce, and everything else.

When Mayflower was here at the house, we would often go on rides through the woods that extended for some miles behind my home. It would usually be late afternoon when I got home from work. As I'd walk to the barn, Mayflower would run up to me and nicker (kind of a cross between a snort and sneeze).

I would brush her down good and she would almost go to sleep. (I respond the same way to similar activity.) The smell of saddle leather and hay combined with the vision of slanted sunrays slipping through the walls of the old barn created a calmness—a tranquility that comes from familiarity, a contentment that comes from silence.

Back then, Mayflower and I shared a friendship with a dog named Chip. Chip was a product of impeccable breeding—the result of lust between a registered Labrador Retriever and a dashing hound of unknown origin. Chip, Mayflower, and I would leave the confines of the barn and pasture on those afternoons on a quest to find ... ? Adventure has no defined course or destination.

The road that led through the woods was a two-rutted lane lined on both sides by a mixture of pine trees and sweetgum. Some seedlings clung to the edge of the little ditch that ran along the side of the road, as a trickle of water slipped slowly and silently past. The trees were fairly young saplings, having taken seed after the field had last been harvested nearly thirty years ago. Pine needles covered the ground under the trees, and a sprinkling of spikey gum balls created a cover like an auburn-colored chenille bed spread.

The three of us proceeded through the woods one afternoon on an undetermined quest. We in no way looked like a triumvirate from a medieval story. While Mayflower was nothing like a prancing charger, she was much more elegant than Don Quixote's Rocinante. And I was certainly no knight in shining armor. Unlike the Spanish nobleman, I was clad in a flannel shirt, jeans, and boots. Still, our quest was noble nonetheless.

As we proceeded through the woods, Chip (the Sancho Panza of this trio) would occasionally run off by himself in search of unknown quarry. In a short time, he would reappear, panting from the effort and pleased to rejoin us.

At some point, I decided to take the path less traveled, turned off the wooded road, and began to wind among the trees. I brushed the hanging pine boughs away as we proceeded through the older forest. Many of the trees in this part of the woods had been here for half a century or more, having survived somehow the saws and axes of the timber crews that had been so much a part of the lumber industry in this area. The limbs spread out and created a canopy that generated a shadowy filigree of light as the sun began to go down. Mayflower stepped adroitly over fallen branches, occasionally snapping small twigs.

In a few minutes, we came out into an open area, a dormant field. The late afternoon sun lit the old field with rays of sunshine that burst through the trees. There stood a large oak tree, oddly placed among all the pines. I dismounted and went over to that tree, then sat down beside it with my back against its trunk. I let Mayflower's reins drop as she stood with her head down beside me. Chip came over and put his big head in my lap. I heard a bird skipping through the leaves and became swept up in peacefulness.

Then I heard the sound of traffic, of trucks and cars as they passed down the four-lane highway only a couple hundred yards away. The sound did not diminish the moment. Instead, the sudden contrast enhanced the sense of peace I had found. But it was more than a sense, more than a feeling. The reaction was visceral: my body relaxed as the breeze blew and the sun dimmed behind the trees. At that moment, the sound of the modern world was excluded from my mind, erased by the reality of what I had discovered.

Miss Esther and the Hush Puppies

I have written about Miss Esther in other publications, particularly those that have to do with the South, or, at least, our perception of the South. Miss Esther Camaron was a Southern Lady, though she didn't fit any of the ordinary stereotypes folks often associate with the term. I may have used a different name in writing about her sometimes, but the real Miss Esther was unique.

Esther Camaron was very proud, but she had a kind of exuberant gentility that put those around her at ease. Her soothing nature always came through during her non-stop narratives about recent community activities, or descriptions of encounters at the grocery store, a church service, or a Woman's Club or garden club meeting. Those narratives were often accompanied by waving of hands and intimations of knowledge unknown to the rest of the world, as well as instructions not to repeat any part of what she'd just said. Miss Esther loved to laugh and loved to make others laugh. That laughter sometimes belied a certain toughness that allowed her to rise above what could have been otherwise depressing circumstances.

Back in the early 1950s, my family owned a small oil distributorship as part of our general store in Hallsboro. Most of our business was providing fuel to farmers in the summer to fire their tobacco curers, and in the winter we provided home heating oil, either kerosene or fuel oil. Miss Esther was one of our winter customers.

She lived in a big, two-story house that, at one time, had been a real showplace. It was kept up nicely, but it had deteriorated some since its heyday back in the '20s. The Great Depression had adversely affected her family's finances and, subsequently, her husband had become a salesman for a local retail company. He had died right after World War II, and Miss Esther had never held what she called a "public job." Her sole source of revenue came from work as a substitute English teacher, and sometimes she would rent a room to "just the right kind" of tenant. Miss Esther was also very frugal.

Even in her diminished financial situation, Miss Esther never lost her sense of "respectability"—the dignity of her perceived place in society—while still maintaining her ability to make everyone she met feel as if they were the most important person in her life at that particular time. In essence, she never stopped being a lady.

Each fall, Miss Esther would call the oil plant and remind us it was time to fill her oil tank. I was usually the one to make the delivery, and there would almost always be some small maintenance of her heating equipment involved. One particular visit lingers in my memory.

The year was about 1960 or so. Miss Esther had a very elegant dining room with a large fireplace at one end. She had covered the fireplace opening with a sheet of blue-painted plywood with a hole cut in it to accommodate a tin flue from a free-standing oil heater. On that particular delivery day, she wanted me to fit the flue through the wooden cover. I told her I'd have to put a flue collar on it to keep the wood from touching the hot flue. This did not fit into Miss Esther's esthetic ideals. She had painted the flue and the wood a dark blue, so she instructed me to paint the collar dark blue. Using the paint and brush she supplied, I painted the collar that she had previously chosen not to use, simply because it "didn't look good."

After I had painted the collar, I filled the fuel tank and installed the flue and new collar. Upon review, Miss Esther concluded that the blue on the collar was not exactly the shade of blue that she had wanted to match the blue plywood and, more importantly, the blue satin upholstery of the dining room chairs. I assured her that when the paint dried, it would match. She said, "Well, William, it is tea time anyway, so why don't we have a bit of tea while we wait for the paint to dry?"

I was standing there with oil and soot all over me, but I knew better than to spurn Miss Esther's invitation. So, I washed up at the sink on the back porch. When I returned to the dining room, my hostess had placed a silver tray and two glasses of iced tea on the table. She said, "Now, William, I have some chocolate cookies or some of those little crackers if you would like, but I thought we might share a few of these hush puppies I fixed yesterday."

So, we did. Miss Esther and I sat there for quite a while, talking about my plans for college. The substitute English teacher and I talked about Emily Dickenson and Walt Whitman and Thoreau and Shakespeare. Then she talked about her family's reflections on "the War"—an interchangeable term for "the War of Northern Aggression"—and World Wars I and II. She talked about her grandfather who had fought in the Confederate army and come back home to build up the family farm, and how the other wars had changed her life as well.

Every war had taken family members away. In many cases, those who fought and died were the primary providers for the family. Their passing meant "planned marriages," sale of properties, or "farming out" of children to other family members as everyone adjusted to their new lives.

When we had finished our tea, hush puppies, and conversation, Miss Esther concluded that the flue collar needed another coat of paint. I applied it and she was satisfied.

C

I was not the only young person to come under the spell of Miss Esther.

For a while, she rented a room at her house to carefully chosen tenants. One was a young man, named Johnny Hope, who worked at Boys Home, which was right across the street from Miss Esther's house.

One summer, my sister Linda worked at Boys Home and made an acquaintance of the young man who had rented the room in the old house. Naturally, since Linda was and is an attractive girl, Johnny asked Linda to go on a date. Of course, I don't know much about the date itself, but I do remember Linda telling me about her visit to Miss Esther's house. While there, Linda received very specific instructions on how a lady was supposed to act when visiting the residence of a young man. Miss Esther had given said information freely without request or urging:

A young lady was not to go into the young man's room.

The young man would always introduce guests to Miss Esther.

A young lady must always be introduced as "Miss," and Miss Esther must be made aware of the young lady's familial background.

A specific time was given as to the young man's return.

The young man would walk his date to the door before leaving her at her home.

C

My life has been well-populated with ladies like Miss Esther, women who put a premium on dignity and decorum. Some might think such qualities are superficial, of little substance, or reflect attitudes that are outdated. Those same people might not find guidelines of interaction to be virtuous but rather reflections of a time and place that no longer exists. Miss Esther was a product of time and place, and that is not a bad thing. Despite what modern doyennes may think, the ability to make others feel comfortable—to be hospitable in an often indifferent, cold world—never goes out of style. To make that happen, we need some guidelines. Rules of etiquette, good manners, are just guidelines to help us interact more easily with each other.

Miss Esther gave all who knew her a roadmap to follow on the path to a more harmonious relationship with others. I probably ought to write her a thank you note, but it wouldn't be proper after all this time. Then again, Miss Esther taught us that an act of kindness or gratitude is always proper.

Miss Esther moved from the old house some time ago and has since died. The building eventually fell into ruin. Since then I've eaten a lot of hush puppies, but it's never been quite the same.

A Ride in
Miss Hattie's Wagon

I parked the car in the shade of a giant old water oak whose branches spread out over the back and side of the house. As I stepped out of the car, I felt the slightest breeze stir the leaves of the tree and heard crickets chirp their evening prelude. Other than that, there was a stillness and a silence that was comforting, a calmness that absorbed the modern sounds and activity I had just left. For just a minute, I thought if I moved, it would break the spell.

They had said the governor was coming to visit during that summer of 2016, so I thought I'd go out to Pine Log Plantation prior to his visit to see what he was going to see. The owners were friends of mine, and they had suggested I go see the old place as they'd begun restoring it. I'd heard a lot about the restoration and had intended to go sooner, but I just hadn't got around to it.

I had waited until early evening to go out there in order to miss some of the extreme heat of the summer day. I was partially successful. It was not quite as hot as previously, but the humidity was oppressive. I could see a little mist rising from the swamp as I crossed the bridge over Pine Log Branch, west of Whiteville, and just before I got to the house.

As I pulled into the driveway, I noted this wasn't a typical Southern plantation, at least, not the stereotypical mansion like Tara in *Gone with the Wind.* It was a much more realistic depiction of the kinds of plantations that had existed in the South in the nineteenth century: a working farm where the family had labored alongside the hired hands and slaves (if they'd had any), and life was not so much a series of parties as it was daily care of the crops in the fields.

The main house was a comfortable looking residence with a wide porch across the front, the kind of porch made for sitting in contemplation or watching the train pass just across the road, for shelling butterbeans or just sharing conversation with family and friends. Although the plantation dated back to 1854, the present house hadn't been built until 1880. Mr. Chester Watkins had also built a general store across the road back about 1900. The store building was no longer there, but it was easy to imagine folks in the area coming to buy groceries or dry goods or other supplies they couldn't make or grow at home. Pine Log Plantation had been the kind of place neighbors told visitors about—the kind of place that had become a point of pride for the community. Back then, everybody knew the Watkins family.

There was nobody else on the place that day, so I decided I'd take an unguided tour. I had been to the plantation once before, prior to all the work being done to restore it. A lot had changed. As I walked toward the old chicken house, I wondered about the brick fence built around the chicken yard—must have been some really robust chickens to need a fence that strong!

I could see the family cemetery up a slight hill just past the barn and stables. I thought I'd check it out before the sunlight reduced the visibility, making the tombstones hard to read. I walked past a shed, under which sat various types of antique farm equipment, and I had just passed the end of the barn when I heard the unmistakable creak and rattle of a wooden wagon behind me. When I turned around, I saw what seemed like something from another time and place, a memory come to life.

It was, indeed, a wagon I had heard. It was pulled by a mule, his brown coat flaked with dust as he slowly emerged from the doorway of the barn. The driver was a stocky woman who wore a green print dress and rubber boots that came up to her knees: a unique fashion statement to say the least. I figured she was a docent or a guide hired as part of the effort to recreate the plantation. In keeping with the realistic recreation, she was not wearing a long gown or twirling a parasol, as would have been the case at Tara.

This was not another Southern belle.

"You lookin' for something, mister?" she asked, a slight scowl on her face.

"No, ma'am," I said. "Just wanted to take a look around. I hear the governor's coming. Just wanted to see what he's going to see."

"I ain't heard nothin' about the governor comin'. What's he comin' for?" Her voice was rough, a country voice, much harsher than Miss O'Hara's.

"Just visiting the area. See this beautiful place. Maybe raise some money. Political visit, you know," I offered.

"Well, I ain't got time for politics. Got better things to do. Fact is, I'm behind right now. Get in this wagon if you wanta see the place. Might put you to work so I can catch up some. Name's Hattie, by the way."

So began a wonderful journey guided by one of the most unique individuals I have ever met. As Hattie and I rode the wagon down through the watery branch, she told me stories of Pine Log Plantation.

"Used to be a grist mill right along here," she said as we started across a small, reconstructed bridge. "Fact is, there was two mills: one for corn and one for wheat. Mostly we done the millin' for ourselves, but did some for neighbors too. Got to where it was pretty good money one time. Had a buncha dams built up back through here and way up the swamp; helped control the flow of water to run the mills. Kind of a complicated system that took a lot of lookin' after. 'Course, you know the weather around here is awful changeable and no matter how much attention you pay, sometimes it'll just overcome you. Happened when we'd have a lot of rain or if one of them hurricanes come up. The dams would bust and flood everything. I remember one time when the water washed away everything but the house, and the old pack house, and chicken coop by where the apartment is now. But we never quit, you know. We just fixed up and kept on goin'."

Miss Hattie didn't speak for a while as she maneuvered the mule and wagon through some muddy paths and around cypress stumps. Water splashed as the mule plodded down the watery path. A snake slithered out of the way. In the light that filtered through the filigree of moss on the cypress trees, I saw bright flashes of flowers, lilies, and wild wisteria, growing on little islands throughout the swamp. Egrets and ducks had tucked themselves away for the night among the palmettos and bay trees.

"Used to do a lot of huntin' and fishin' back in here too," said Hattie. "Mostly it was for food, but every once in a while we'd have folks from Wilmington or down in South Carolina come up here and stay for a while just for the fun of it. 'Course, we charged 'em for the hospitality. Ain't nothin' free, you know."

Just as Miss Hattie turned off the swampy road onto an even swampier path, I heard the roar of a bull alligator. "A lot of them around?" I asked.

"Yeah, I reckon. But if you don't bother them, they won't bother you," she replied.

Then Hattie stopped the wagon, got down, and walked a few feet over to a clearing. She took wide, short steps that helped to navigate the wet ground. In the clearing was a small moonshine still with several large glass containers full of clear, illegal alcohol. "C'mon and make yourself useful. Take them jars and put 'em in the wagon," she directed. Some of the jars were gallon size and some were bigger. Hattie handled them all easily.

"Don't act like you ain't never seen moonshine before. Everybody 'round here knows we been makin' and sellin' this since the Civil War. We sold to the Yankees and the Rebs. Good thing we did sell some to the Yankees since Confederate money weren't worth nothin' after the war. Fact that it's good stuff kept folks comin' back. When the Depression and all that come, we survived. You know, people will find money for somethin' they want, even if they have to do without somethin' they need. The booze never let us down. Cotton and tobacco just weren't all that dependable, and the store couldn't compete with the town stores."

"How did you escape the law?" I asked.

"Well, we didn't always. Some of my kin spent time in the pen for sellin' this stuff. Even had one of my ancestors go to jail for killin' a man; a black man I believe it was that he killed." She sat down on the back of the wagon, looking off through the swamp. Miss Hattie's face was tanned almost up to her hairline, indicating that she had probably worn a bonnet to ward of the hot sun. Wrinkles flowed like streams across her forehead and down her cheeks. She wasn't a beautiful woman, but her eyes still sparkled with a softness that belied her age and the hard life she had led.

"Life's been rough. Sometimes some piddlin' drunk would come up to the house, and I'd have to pull a gun on 'im to keep 'im from killin' me, 'cause he wanted that booze but didn't have no money. This plantation has been in my family too long to give it up when hard times come. Sometimes I had to do things other folks didn't think was 'proper.' But proper don't buy no groceries."

After we loaded the jars in the wagon, Miss Hattie aimed the mule back through the swampland we had just come through. *What a remarkable woman,* I thought. *She has survived through a tumultuous time, had experiences that would defeat most people, but, as she said, she "just fixed up and kept on goin'."*

I wondered exactly what had kept her going, what kind of personal life she lead. "You ever been married, Miss Hattie?" I asked.

"Now, that's an impolite question to ask a lady you just met!" she replied. "But just for your information ..." she paused and then smiled mysteriously, "I didn't ever need a husband. There was plenty of men callers, and I could pretty much take care of myself." For just a brief moment, I thought of Miss Scarlett in a green print dress and rubber boots.

We were almost back to the main house when we drove past the restored tobacco barn. What had once been the means of curing the predominate crop in that part of the country had been converted into a place where folks could come and cook outside and have some cold refreshments. Come to think of it, folks had always done that when tobacco was cured there too.

"You go ahead and get out right here," Miss Hattie said abruptly as we stopped just past the tobacco barn. "I'm going to put my booze in a secret room where that apartment is now. You don't need to know where it is."

I stepped down off the wagon and thanked Miss Hattie for my tour. I watched her briefly as she drove away. Then I noticed the sun was still shining. It seemed we had been on the tour a long time, but time had stood still. The summer heat had abated, though the sun was shining as brightly enough for me to read the letters on a tombstone behind me in the cemetery. A wayward breeze blew leaves across one of the markers that lay flat on the ground, revealing the epitaph:

HATTIE MAE WATKINS
DAUGHTER OF CHESTER
AND BRUCE WATKINS
1894-1959

I looked around for the mule and wagon, but they were gone.

Singing with Susans

Over the years, I have been pleased to sing with a lot of people who were much better singers than me. A lot of those performers were young women who happened to be beautiful and talented. Most of them were former or reigning Miss North Carolina winners.

For many years, the city of Charlotte held a holiday celebration called Carolinas Carrousel, with the biggest event being a spectacular parade down Tryon Street, the main street trough the downtown area. (The parade has since been rebranded as the Novant Health Thanksgiving Day Parade.) Of course, the festivities also included a pageant to select the Carrousel Queen.

In 1976, I was asked to sing as part of the entertainment for the pageant the night before the parade. The main attraction for the pageant was the reigning Miss North Carolina, Susan Lawrence. She was one of the most beautiful women I have ever seen. She was taller than most women, about five foot seven. She had dark brown hair, sparkling brown eyes; a fair, smooth complexion; and a smile that lit it all up. I still say that after observing beautiful women in hundreds of pageants around the country. She also had a beautiful voice, as I learned when she sang at the pageant. That night was the first time Susan and I had met, but we almost immediately became friends. We had a lot in common: music, pageants, traveling around North Carolina, and even a few mutual friends.

The next day, after the parade, there was to be a tree lighting ceremony in Marshall Park, which was right across the street from the hotel where all the Carrousel guests were staying. As is often the case in North Carolina, the weather took an unexpected turn during the night, and snow covered the ground the morning of the ceremony. Regardless of the weather, the officials decided to proceed with the tree lighting ceremony, which included Miss North Carolina singing some carols prior to the lighting.

After some conversation with the officials, it was determined the only equipment in the lighting area other than a switch to turn on the lights was one microphone. This was before the days of taped accompaniment, so the piano that would have been there to accompany Susan was not going to be placed in the inclement weather. She would have to sing a cappella.

Noting the absence of technical support, Susan asked if I would sing some of the carols with her. I had planned to just watch as a guest that morning, but of course, I agreed. So, Susan and I stood next to the Christmas tree in the snow and cold, and we sang some familiar Christmas carols. Only a few people stood in front of the little stage. Most of them were members of the Carrousel committee. It was not the kind of "crowd" that would make an entertainer want to give their greatest performance. But Susan sang as if she were in an major auditorium with thousands in attendance.

I don't remember all the specific carols, but I know we sang "Let It Snow." Then, the people who had joined us in the cold began to sing with us. The weather was frightening, but the spirit warmed us all. Susan stood there like a queen leading her subjects. Of course, she wore her Miss North Carolina crown and was swathed in a fur coat. She could have said, "I don't want to go out in this weather. It will ruin my voice." But she didn't do that. She went out and did her duty as any queen would do. The people there watched a beautiful, talented woman perform under adverse circumstances when she really didn't have to. I think they appreciated that. I certainly did.

We all have Christmas images that stick in our memories, but one of my favorites is singing with Susan that day. Over the years, I have sung with a lot of people in a wide variety of circumstances, and although that occasion was most unusual, the most memorable part for me was getting to meet a most remarkable woman.

We never sang together again, although we were part of many occasions where we sang separately. Susan was always gracious to everybody she met, always went the extra mile to please folks who came to see her. She never seemed to set herself apart. I later asked her to be a part of the Boys Home Christmas television program and she accepted, donating her time and talent. When she came to visit my home in Lake Waccamaw, my daughter, just six years old at the time, fell in love with her. Susan accompanied us to church for the Sunday morning service and endeared herself to all the church members.

I guess the reason I included Susan in this collection of memorable people is because she was one of the first beauty queens I met. Prior to meeting Susan, I had a nebulous notion that beauty queens were all about being pretty. Most of that impression came from watching the Miss America Pageant on television, an impersonal perception at best. But Susan allowed me to get to know her, to learn that she had been a kind of tomboy more involved in playing high school basketball than modeling evening gowns. She made me see beyond the outward beauty that was so obvious, to the real Susan who loved people, who genuinely cared about what was going on, not only in the big cities of America but also in the little towns like her own Midway. Susan set the standard I would, from that point, use to determine who a real beauty queen should be. I don't know if any of the many other queens I met ever fully met Susan's standard, but, for the most part, they worked toward that end.

Susan Lawrence had qualified to compete in the Miss North Carolina Pageant by winning the Miss Thomasville Pageant just a few months earlier. She went on to become the first runner-up to Miss America for 1976. Ironically, she had been crowned Miss North Carolina by another Susan who had come from another furniture-making town just down the road from Thomasville.

Susan Griffin had been Miss High Point before she won the state title in 1974. Miss Griffin was also one of those women who combined beauty with a showstopping voice. Her signature song, the one that had made her a talent winner in the Miss America Pageant, was "With a Song in My Heart." Nobody had ever sung it better.

Susan Griffin later married Cole Fisher from Elizabethtown, just a few miles from my hometown of Hallsboro. Through the years, this Susan and I also became friends, and, although we didn't live far apart, we never sang together until 1987, when we were asked to sing for the ladies' luncheon at the Optimist International Convention in Charlotte. As the name implies, Optimist is a service organization, its clubs located all around the world, particularly in the United States and Canada. That year, over 3,500 members attended the gathering in Charlotte.

I don't really know how many ladies were at the luncheon. I do know that the convention center was full and I was the only man in attendance. We had put together a little program that involved me singing a few songs, then Susan would sing some songs, then we'd sing some together, and we would close with a duet arrangement of *An American Trilogy*. The song is a medley of "Dixie", an old folk song called "All My Sorrows", and ends with "Battle Hymn of the Republic".

We had received a warm response from the ladies and felt good about the show as we started the finale. As I began to sing "Dixie", I could see beyond the spotlights as ladies began to stand and sing the Southern anthem along with me. I was a little surprised. After all, the song had been banned from football stadiums and other public gatherings due to its association with the Confederacy. Susan joined me in the little folk song and then when we got to the "Battle Hymn of the Republic", the whole convention center was standing and singing.

The audience that day was made up of women from all over the world: different races, different religions, different creeds, all kinds of different backgrounds. But for just a little while, in the convention center in Charlotte, they sang as one voice, together singing an anthem that proclaimed unity, a song that soared above differences.

When the song ended, the applause began and went on for a long time. After we left the stage, I hugged Susan. We were so swept up in the moment that neither of us spoke. I had never been so moved by anything before.

Susan left and I found myself out in the hallway of the convention center. As I was walking out, a lady come up to me and took me by the arm and said, "We showed 'em, didn't we? We're just all one country. Thank you."

I tell this story to point out that sometimes individuals can redefine stereotypes. Both Susans were beauty queens. But those who stood in the snow in downtown Charlotte back in 1976, and the ladies who rose to sing in the convention center years later, didn't just see beauty queens. I think the women in the audience saw how the women on stage were much like themselves, real people, with all the preconceptions and stereotypes of beauty queens washed away. If they were wrong about beauty queens, could they be wrong about who their neighbors were, or what their role was in their community, or what undeveloped talent they each might be hiding or … ?

I don't think either Susan thought about the effect she had on her audience. Those women were just being themselves and sharing themselves with other people. So many people think of beauty queens and pageants as shallow images of what we ought to be. But if such events can help develop more Susans in this world, I'm all for it.

Nick Boddie: More Than Just a Nice Guy

One Easter Saturday, in the late 1960s, snow began to fall around lunchtime. Snow anytime in North Carolina is a rarity, but it's a real shock in the spring and particularly if you're showing horses in an outdoor arena. I had gone to Raeford, North Carolina, to participate in a little quarter horse show held at a farm there. I had just one horse and a little trailer. When the show management decided to delay, hoping the snow would stop, I put the horse back in the trailer and prepared to wait out the delay. I wasn't ready for the cold, and there was no heater in the old pickup truck I was driving. Fortunately, I met a nice guy who invited me to share his heated camper. Back in those days, big rigs, multi-horse trailers with living quarters, and RVs were not very common. So, when the gentleman offered his camper as a refuge from the weather, I readily accepted.

The kind gentleman's name was Nick Boddie. He was at the show with his wife, Betsy, and two young daughters, Bryan and Anne. The girls were very active and strong youth competitors. If I remember correctly, my horse and I didn't do very well in that show (snowflakes tended to hamper performances), but meeting Nick and his family was one of the best things to happen in my life.

At that time, Nick, his brother Mayo, and their uncle, Carleton Noell, had just founded a new company called Boddie-Noell Enterprises in Rocky Mount, North Carolina. That company would become one of the largest Hardee's franchisors in the country and expand into other areas, making Nick a very wealthy man.

That day marked the beginning of a long friendship that I value highly to this day. As executive vice-president of Boddie-Noell, Nick would go on to lead one of the most successful businesses in the country, but, for me, and just about everybody else he met, Nick stayed the same humble, fun-loving man I met at that horse show.

Nick's story is not exactly a rags-to-riches tale, but it is a story of determination, hard work, and an approach to business that gives a whole new meaning to "family business."

Sometime after the horse show in Raeford, I went to work with Boys Homes of North Carolina at Lake Waccamaw. One of the first people I suggested for membership on the board of trustees was Nick. Fortunately, he agreed to serve and did so until his death in 2011. Over those fifty or so years, I had a chance to talk with Nick often about Boys and Girls Homes, horses, business, family, and a wide range of other topics—including his road to success.

As we sat for dinner one night at the Carleton House, a restaurant owned by Boddie-Noell in Rocky Mount, Nick told me about how his father had lost their farm in Nash County and moved to Rocky Mount during the Great Depression. They had done a lot of different things just to make ends meet: they sold chickens and eggs, cut pulpwood, and pumped gas. Nick had even worked for a while, laying track for a railroad in Alaska. "I thought we had mosquitos in North Carolina until I went to Alaska," he told me once. "Swarms of them would cover us in the summer."

Nick had graduated from Rocky Mount High School and attended one year of college before coming back home to work at a hotel his aunt owned. Eventually, he, his brother Mayo, and Uncle Carlton Noell had bought the Carleton House, and it became a premier eating establishment in town. Then a former school mate presented them with an opportunity to buy into the recently formed Hardee's fast food franchise. Fast food was a fairly new concept in the '60s. The idea of selling hamburgers for thirty-five cents didn't have an immediate appeal. However, after they had watched the first stores become successful, the brothers and their uncle built their first Hardee's restaurant in Fayetteville, North Carolina.

"We did a pretty good business 'til a McDonald's opened down the street. Sales fell off but came back, and we built another store in Kinston and then a second store in Fayetteville," he said.

Boddie-Noell Enterprises grew to be the largest Hardee's franchisor in the country, and they later expanded their business to include real estate development. Their business plan was pretty simple: provide personal attention and treat employees like family. That paternal approach may have been hard to maintain with 10,000 employees, but it must have worked; their company boasted many twenty-year employees in an industry with an average turnover of less than a year.

The primary factor that separated Nick from a lot of other successful businessmen was his genuine interest in the people who worked for him. He made it a point to meet each employee personally. He would ask about their family, how things were going at that particular establishment, and generally make them feel like they were an essential part of the business. And they were. Nick realized that and made sure every person knew it.

Over the years, I'd meet Nick for lunch at one of his various restaurants. At least once a year, Nick would have me come up to Rocky Mount to speak to his Optimist Club about Boys and Girls Homes, and he once arranged for Boys and Girls Homes to receive all the income from the sale of French fries in one day at Boddie-Noell's Hardee's stores. He made a lot of other monetary contributions, but what made the greatest impression on the kids at the home was when Nick would arrive on campus in his helicopter. The children would rush outside to see him land, and he would greet them individually.

One little boy named Lucky was bold enough to ask Nick to take him up in the helicopter. Nick had the pilot take Lucky and a staff member for a quick trip over the lake while Nick was in a meeting. Years later, when Lucky graduated from high school, he invited Nick to his graduation ceremony. Nick came early on the afternoon of the ceremony and took Lucky on another helicopter ride. Lucky never forgot Nick.

You don't meet too many men in the course of life who are as selfless as Nick Boddie. He was a man who had the resources to do whatever he wanted and didn't have to do much he didn't want to do. He *chose* to help others.

Perhaps the biggest beneficiary of Nick's love for kids was the Boy Scouts. He was an Eagle Scout, and that program had remained a big part of his life. He kept all of the Scout Law: trustworthiness, loyalty, helpfulness, friendship, courteousness, kindness, obedience, cheer, thrift, bravery, cleanliness, and reverence. But most importantly, Nick was his own man who always did what he thought was right and best for himself, his family, and his neighbors, whether it was giving of his time or money, or offering a cold cowboy a respite from the spring snow.

Editors and Publishers and Such

Per the advice of my college advisor, Dr. Paul Yoder, I decided to pursue a degree in something other than music; I chose English. I thought it would give me a broad background to pursue a multitude of careers—and it did. For over fifty years, I have been writing *something:* straight news stories, feature stories, short stories, novels, hundreds of magazine articles, corporate communications (speeches, board reports, newsletters, appeal letters, etc.), and even some ad copy. In the process, I have had the benefit (or misfortune) of working with some incredible people who helped transfer my thoughts to paper or television or radio.

When I started work at Boys and Girls Homes in the mid 1960s, one of my first assignments was to re-design and write a newsletter to send out to all the regular contributors to keep them up-to-date on activities on the campus. Mrs. Hester McCray had previously written a version of the newsletter. When Mr. McCray, her husband and my boss, assigned that job to me, Mrs. McCray was told to assist and educate me. She had been an English teacher for many years prior to coming to Lake Waccamaw.

When she reviewed my drafts for the newsletter, she conducted my tutorial in the same manner as she had graded her students' papers. She would return my attempts many times, often changing parts she had already changed. Eventually, as deadlines approached, Mr. McCray would say, "That's it, Florence (his nickname for Mrs. Hester McCray), we got to go to press."

One of my other duties for Boys Home was to write scripts for numerous slide presentations. In those days, before PowerPoint or other presentation software, we used a slide tray of photographs and played a recorded narration to go with it. I later used that experience to get a job writing and producing television programs which in turn led me, circuitously, to writing my first newspaper columns.

In the course of doing news stories and feature stories for the *Carolina in the Morning* television show on WECT in Wilmington, I would come across subjects that just begged for further personal interpretation. So, in 1981 I approached Thom Billington, then editor, and publisher Jim High, of the *News Reporter* in Whiteville, about starting a column. After some discussion, Jim said, "Let's give it a try." They agreed to run my column, initially entitled *Dateline: Redbug,* once a week in the bi-weekly paper. Thom was a tough journalist whose primary concern was news, *real news,* not "fluff stuff." But he encouraged me to continue my columns and to even seek publication in other papers. So, being a staunch believer in the personal approach to everything, I took samples of my columns to newspaper editors all over North and South Carolina, accompanied by what may have been the most tentative letter of support ever written. Thom's letter of introduction to the prospective publishers said, "Bill Thompson writes a better-than-average column for our paper." Those folks who knew Thom understood that such a statement was high praise coming from a man whose journalistic standards were difficult to meet. When I turned in my columns, hard-news Thom often asked, jokingly, "You got anything relevant this week?"

I continued to write that column for over twenty years, learning something from each of the editors of the thirty different papers who paid me the large sum of five dollars for each column. The major lesson I learned from all those daily, weekly, and bi-weekly newspaper editors was: "Our papers print local news." I guess they considered my columns local news; I wrote about people and activities that were relatable to people in just about every small town in the Carolinas. I appreciated the compliments from readers who said, "I liked your column last week. I used to know somebody just like that" or "I told somebody just the other day the same thing you said in the paper last week." I even appreciated those "other" comments: "You ought not to make fun of Yankees. They liable to quit coming down here and I need their money." But when a reader who recently transplanted from New Jersey requested a few seeds to plant a grits tree like the one I talked about in a column, it was hard to resist a little teasing.

Arlene Gutterman wasn't an editor. She was an advertising representative for *Our State* magazine, and she was the one who presented samples of my newspaper columns to Mary Ellis Best, Elizabeth Hudson, and Bernie Mann at *Our State*. Boys and Girls Homes had run an ad in the magazine (courtesy of Nick Boddie), and I mentioned my column to Arlene one day when she was in our office. Mary was the editor, Elizabeth was associate editor, and Bernie was the publisher of the new magazine that was making a real splash in homes all across North Carolina. Bernie had bought an old magazine called *The State* and revamped it into a modern publication that reflected the people and culture of the Old North State. Mary and Elizabeth had helped that effort by getting some of the best writers in the state to write for the magazine. So, when Mary called me after reading some of my material that Arlene had given her, I was flattered. She asked me to meet with her and Elizabeth in Greensboro to discuss writing for the magazine.

That meeting was the beginning of a long, wonderful relationship with the people of *Our State*. I wrote the humor column, *Front Porch Stories,* for over a decade and followed that with a series of individual profiles called *Bill Thompson's Carolina Characters* as well as some feature stories. I mentioned to Mary and Elizabeth that the first freelance writing for which I'd been paid was a piece I'd written for *The State* back in about 1966 or '67. Somehow, the ladies found a copy of that story about an old mule standing in the rain, mulling over the demise of his reign as a primary element in farming. I showed the story to Bernie who commented, "You haven't changed your style or subject matter much." That was true then.

Still is.

Bernie Mann was a smart businessman. He had a background in broadcasting that had helped him gain a considerable amount of expertise in what it took to promote any kind of enterprise. He also had a basic philosophy of entrepreneurship that he applied to every project he was involved in: "If it doesn't make money, drop it." Mann Media, the corporate entity that owned *Our State*, at one point tried to develop another magazine similar to *Our State* but aimed at a younger audience. Suffice to say, it failed. But *Our State* became, and continues to be, one the most successful regional publications in the country.

Bernie also started another venture into the publishing business: book publishing. Our State Books became an extension of Mann Media's effort to promote North Carolina by printing books by North Carolina authors about topics related to the South, North Carolina in particular. Bernie chose Mary Best to head up the new enterprise. For Mary, it was just another challenge that she took on with great enthusiasm and boundless energy. She had not had any previous book publishing experience, but she sought the advice of a lot of people who had and used that information to build the business.

I was one of the first people Mary asked about writing a book for the new publishing venture. When she first suggested we do a book comprised of essays much like the *Front Porch Stories* column, I thought she meant we would do a compilation of some of the columns previously printed in the magazine. But she wanted *all new* stories and essays. That was a whole different project! I went to work, and the result was my first book, *Sweet Tea, Fried Chicken and Lazy Dogs: Reflections on North Carolina Life.* (The title was suggested by Amy Jo Wood, the director of marketing for *Our State*.) It turned out to be an unexpected bestseller for Mann Media, with over 40,000 in sales.

The main reason the book was so successful was the great promotional campaign Our State Books did. The company ran ads in the magazine; had me do book signings at bookstores, libraries, and book festivals; promoted speaking engagements; and set up booths at festivals of all kinds. We didn't go to just book festivals. We went to every kind of celebration. Mary, Amy Jo, and I were all new to the book promotion business, so we learned together.

On one occasion, we went to a food festival in Charlotte, not knowing exactly what the situation was to be. We found that we were on our own to promote the book. So, after we hadn't received any traffic at our booth, we took the books out and placed them on some picnic tables. Mary held up a sign with the book's cover, and I stood on the street, shook hands, and literally pulled people in until a group was formed. Then I would start telling stories. I was like a street preacher, spreading the gospel of North Carolina. I loved it! And we sold a lot of books that day.

We followed my first book with *Pearl's Pork Palace and Other Stories from Flynn's Crossing, North Carolina.* (We liked long titles.) That was a collection of short stories written in the first person by folks in the fictional town of Flynn's Crossing. While that book was successful, it wasn't a best seller like *Sweet Tea*. So, we went back to the essay format with *Backyards, Bowties and Beauty Queens*. By that time, internet marketing was added to the promotional campaign, so that book sold well also.

During this time, 2004 or so, Mary got married and moved to South Carolina, where she continued to work for the book publishing company. But after about ten years, Mann Media decided to get out of the book publishing business, which was changing at a rapid pace. Mary later went to work for a trade magazine, and I continued to write my columns for *Our State* with the support of the magazine's editors, Vickie Jarrett and Elizabeth Hudson. Mary also continued to introduce me to other magazines that were interested in running my kind of stories.

I guess you could say I got hooked on writing books. But I had never written a novel. Mann Media never was in the business of publishing fiction, other than *Pearl's Pork Palace*. So, I decided I would write a novel and try to find somebody to publish it. The story I had in mind was based on the life of my Grandfather Council. It would be a story of political intrigue during the gubernatorial campaign of 1924, the booming lumber industry in southeastern North Carolina, and the personal challenges of a young man facing racial and social relationships of that time and place. The book was classified as historical fiction, a category that sounds like an oxymoron. One reviewer later said the novel had "all the key elements of a Southern novel: race, religion, sex, and politics."

I did research on three of those.

I wrote query letters and sent samples of the story to every publisher I thought might be interested: big ones, little ones, national, and regional. I got a lot of very polite rejections. Then I got an agent and she received the same responses.

Finally, I was attending a book festival in Lumberton, North Carolina, and met a fellow named Mike Simpson, who was just starting a book publishing company. I asked him to read my manuscript; he did and then agreed to publish it. Second Wind Publishing published *Celia Whitfield's Boy*. The book sold relatively well and was one of the publishing company's best-selling books. It was even nominated for the

Sir Walter Raleigh Prize for Fiction, though it wasn't a finalist. Mike was a good man, but he was new in a quickly changing market that was dominated by internet sales and publication. We continued to do a lot of speaking engagements, which resulted in the bulk of our sales. As we went along, internet sales, including Amazon, Barnes and Noble, and others, began to pick up. I went back to my old personal approach and called on a lot of independent bookstores to carry my books. That worked pretty well too.

Despite the success of my novel, I once again thought I'd try something different. Doug Sasser was a friend who lived just down the road from me. He was also a superior court judge, an excellent, award-winning photographer, and a generation younger than me. We came up with the idea of a different kind of coffee table book. We would let Doug's photographs speak for themselves—let them evoke individual responses from the viewers and readers. I would record my responses in the book. The title was a real expression of the content: *Listen to the South Wind.*

I called Mike and asked if he would be interested in publishing such a book. He asked to see some of Doug's photographs. After viewing the photos, he said he would be glad to publish the book under his new imprint, Indigo Sea Press. This was a new kind of project for him as well. Mike was used to the traditional paperback books, trade books. This was a hardcover book in which the color photographs played a major part. It was a challenge to print with the kind of quality such a book required. Mike met the challenge by outsourcing the job. The result was a beautiful book that met the criteria Doug and I had in mind. Still, the book was expensive to produce and difficult to market. As a result, most of the marketing was left to Doug and me, an effort for which neither of us had the time or expertise. It still sold remarkably well under the circumstances. We sold most of the books through Facebook, book signings, and speaking engagements. It is a book we are both proud of but one for which we had greater, maybe unrealistic, expectations.

Although I was disappointed in the sale of *Listen to the South Wind*, I felt I had at least one more book in me. I had spent all those years at Boys and Girls Homes listening to the stories of the children who had come to us from all kinds of backgrounds; they had great stories to tell—and some of them were true! I thought I would tell a story in the manner those children had shared their own stories, stories that stretched the imagination.

I talked to Mike about the storyline of the book, and he agreed to print it. *Chasing Jubal* is the story of two boys from the foothills of Virginia. It is a coming of age story in many ways, but it is also a fantasy that leads the reader through the minds of two men who tell of their adventures as they remember them. It is up to the reader to determine what is true and what is nostalgia and pure fantasy. The book was set in the 1950s, so I didn't have to do a lot of research to fit the story to time and place. The book sold well. It is still in print and available, but I don't think I will write another novel.

The publishing business has changed considerably since I first began writing. Writing books has been one of the greatest experiences of my life. All the other efforts—newspapers, television, magazines, etc.—were fun and, frankly, more financially rewarding. But when I see a book with my name on it, I get a special feeling that is significant to me. It is physical evidence of a lot of hard work, of a creative process that makes me look deep into myself, and that allows me to express my thoughts about a wide variety of topics. Writing is an art, and a book is to a writer what a canvas is to a painter. I like to paint word pictures, and creating those pictures between the covers of a book is a collaborative effort between the publisher, editors, and the writer. I am forever indebted to those publishers and editors who have helped me paint those word pictures. They have guided and educated me so I could be a word painter. I will rely on the folks at PipeVine Press to continue to guide me.

Joe Dale's Boots

*G*rowing up in a small rural community like Hallsboro, you meet a lot of "Joe Dales." They are the seldom seen and seldom heard. They live their lives quietly, routinely. Some might even say their lives are boring. But a life of caring about neighbors, providing for family and serving God and country is not boring. It's being what is known as "good people." I've known a lot of Joe Dales. They are more a part of my life than any famous person I've met. Joe Dale is the everyman that is the heartbeat of life, the pulse of the community. My life would have been different without him.

Joe Dale's boots sat on the edge of the porch. Gray mud had oozed from the leather laces down over the whole boot and on to the wood of the weathered porch. It was a seamless sheet of muck, a combination of dirt and manure and swamp water. The cold wind that swept across the field in front of the house had dried the whole mess, smoothing it out until it looked like it had been sculpted and then welded to the wood. If you'd had a mind to, you could have just picked up the whole thing and set it on top of Joe Dale's tombstone like an unwritten epitaph.

They were the government issue boots Joe Dale had worn when he came home from Korea.

He had worn those boots when he followed our old mule, plowing up the new ground down next to the swamp.

He had worn them when he, Myles Cowan, and Daddy walked across the stubble of the soybean field, watching Ol' Dan with his nose to the ground, looking for quail.

He had worn them when he stood two rows over from the auctioneer as his tobacco crop was auctioned off for the last time at the old warehouse in town.

He had worn them down through the swamp, bumping them against cypress knees when he had to chase the old sow and pigs back up to the broken pen at Uncle Fred's place.

He had worn them when he had to go pick up his son, Joseph, at school when the boy was suspended for smoking cigarettes outside of the school's designated smoking area. Joe Dale had thought that was kind of ironic, seeing as how tobacco had helped pay for the school.

He had worn them when he sorted through what was left of his house and barns after Hurricane Hazel came through, and after, when he and his neighbors rebuilt everything.

He had worn them down to Simmons Mill Pond, where he hardly ever caught any fish but did a lot of quiet relaxing.

He was wearing them when his heart gave out on him as he was coming back from cutting up an old tree for winter firewood over to Miss Ella's house.

Those old muddy boots told a lot about Joe Dale; their frayed laces having woven through the muddy water and dust of his life, tying the insignificant and meaningful together.

EXCERPT FROM *GREEN SWAMP ELEGY* BY BILL THOMPSON.

Winter Fishing
in the Swamp

I
don't remember the exact temperature during the first week in January 1955, but I do remember it was cold enough to freeze the little creek that ran behind our house down on the edge of Bogue Swamp. There had been a little dusting of snow, just enough to close school. The time off gave Clarence Henry and me, just twelve years old at the time, the opportunity to explore the swamp. Clarence said we were "in search of adventure."

Just enough snow had collected on the fallen leaves down by the creek to allow for the creation of footprints but not snowballs. Snow in southeastern North Carolina is not only rare, it is wet and icy— not fluffy—and falls in such miniscule amounts that trying to make snowballs is more like making mud pies.

The swamp and the creek were familiar sites for Clarence and me. We had spent much of our summer trekking through the soft ground, only slightly hampered by protruding cypress knees and ubiquitous palmetto bushes. The summer before that, we had made creative use of upturned stumps of the trees that had been blown over by Hurricane Hazel after the monumental storm descended on our watery playground. The roots stood on edge, thick mud and vines clinging fiercely to their grotesque protrusions that had emerged in the wake of fierce winds and rushing water. In our youthful imaginations, those roots became forts, barricades to hide behind as we assaulted each other with clods of dirt and fired fusillades of imaginary bullets from broken tree limbs crafted by nature to look like rifles.

But that was summertime play. What could two young boys do in a frozen swamp in the winter?

"You reckon we could catch any fish in that creek?" wondered Clarence. He spoke in a voice that changed pitch depending on his enthusiasm for the subject matter. Fishing in a creek, even in the dead of winter, brought out his soprano voice.

"I don't know," I responded. "I read about folks up in Minnesota cuttin' holes in the frozen lakes and catchin' fish through 'em. I reckon fish don't care how cold it gets long as they can find something to eat. Prob'ly not too choosy about what they eat in a froze-over lake since they ain't got a big menu to choose from up north. 'Course, I never have figured out how fish got a taste for worms anyhow. They can't dig 'em up by themselves. Fish ain't got no hands and worms ain't going to jump out of the ground and into the water."

"Well, the creek ain't froze solid nohow. That's just a thin cover," Clarence said as he threw a fallen pine bough into the creek. Its needles weighted down with ice, the limb broke through the thin ice of the creek before quickly sinking into water.

"Hey, I bet I know how we can catch some fish!" Clarence exclaimed. "My Uncle Leroy told me that him and my daddy got a ticket from the game warden for dynamitin' fish. Said they took a stick of dynamite and throwed it in Lake Waccamaw, and it knocked the fish out just like you had hit 'em with a stick. Said they just popped up to the top and you could just scoop 'em off the top of the water with a net."

"I don't know. Never heard of such thing," I said. "Sounds too easy. 'Sides, we ain't got no dynamite."

The pitch of Clarence's speech lowered. "I believe I got something that'll work though," he said as he reached into his jacket pocket. "Right here is something almost as powerful as dynamite: a cherry bomb and a

M80. Some I got left over from shootin' off firecrackers on New Year's Eve last week. These things are powerful! Mama said they was too dangerous to have around. She said Daddy shouldn't have bought 'em since they was illegal and he was settin' a bad example for me. But he let me shoot off some of 'em, and I just kinda held these back after the New Year's celebration. She don't know I got 'em. She'd whip my butt if she knew."

Clarence immediately took out a box of matches, lit the cherry bomb, and tossed it into the creek. The fuse quickly fizzled and lay impotent on the thin ice. With hardly a pause, he took the big M80 and tossed it into the creek. The thin layer of water that had formed over the ice caused that potential explosion to fizzle as well.

"Well, that wont too good of a idea," Clarence said as he looked at the two firecrackers lying dormant on the ice. "Wont fair to the fish anyhow."

1955 was a good year to be twelve years old. Clarence and I were just leaving our "little boyhood." We would soon be teenagers and our lives would go through rapid changes. We would never again be so optimistic, creative, or satisfied with our lives. Fire crackers would never again hold such interest for us. The innocence of childhood is so brief, its value is often lost in the brevity.

Love Story

I first met Mr. Warlick back in the late 1960s when I was speaking to a group at the old Cape Fear Hotel in Wilmington where he worked. Mr. Warlick (Ed was his first name, but I always called him "Mr. Warlick") was in charge of getting the room ready, and he helped adjust the microphone system for me. The hotel was a popular venue for all kinds of meetings that I attended or at which I spoke. Mr. Warlick was always there in his black pants and white shirt with a bow tie. He was in charge of setting up the meeting rooms and was always precise in how the tables and chairs were placed, and if there were food served, he would personally check to make sure each eating utensil was in the right place as well.

Over the years, when I would be at other functions at the hotel, Mr. Warlick and I would speak and eventually we became friends. In the course of our conversations, I learned that he had been born not far from my home in Columbus County. He had met his wife, Elsie, when they were in school together, and they got married just before he left to join the Navy during World War II.

I eventually lost touch with Mr. Warlick until a few days ago, when I was talking with the operator of a nursing home in Wilmington. When she learned I was from Columbus County, she said, "Oh, we had the nicest man and his wife here from Columbus County, Mr. and Mrs. Warlick. Would you know them?"

People always ask me about people from my home county, and I can't possibly know them all, but in this instance, the name rang a bell in my memory. "I used to know a man named Warlick who worked at the old Cape Fear Hotel," I said.

"That's him!" she said. "They came to live with us after Mrs. Warlick had a stroke and Mr. Warlick was unable to care for her at home. They didn't have any children. They were just a wonderful couple."

Then the operator told me a story. Because of her illness, Mrs. Warlick had been in the nursing wing of the facility, and Mr. Warlick had lived in the independent living section. But he had spent every day by her side, even taking his meals with her in her room. Every afternoon, he would roll her in her wheelchair to the little patio area in the center of the building. On Sundays, Mr. Warlick would share a cup of ice cream with his wife. He would feed it to her since Mrs. Warlick was unable to feed herself. He would give her a spoonful and then he would eat a spoonful.

Mr. Warlick told the nursing home operator that he and Elsie had met at a church ice cream social when they were just youngsters, and they'd had a tradition of eating ice cream together every Sunday afternoon since they were married—except for during his time in the military.

After Mrs. Warlick passed away, Mr. Warlick had a small cup of ice cream by himself on the patio every Sunday. He died just a few years ago.

This is a true story, a real ice cream moment, frozen in time.

Billy and Van and Peggy and Carl and Them

Every little town has a café that serves as a gathering point for the community. Not everybody eats every meal there (they just serve breakfast and lunch, of course), but just about everybody will eat there sometime. Gwen's Café is such a place in Hallsboro. The building has been around a long time and the name has changed a few times; even the menu has been updated more than once. But it is still a place where the sense of community resonates among the clatter of dishes, the ring of the cash register, and the conversations between friends who have known each other all their lives.

I had planned to meet Peggy Blanchard and Van Pierce at Gwen's for lunch that Wednesday at noon. I got there a little early and chatted with some of the folks that were already eating. Van arrived a few minutes later and then Peggy rushed in shortly thereafter. We were all old friends, all about the same age, and all of us had grown up in Hallsboro.

Peggy grew up just a couple of doors down from me. She was kinda like an older sister. She once tried to teach me how to dance. It was an unsuccessful effort that resulted in my knocking over a plant on the porch we were dancing on. Peggy was pretty and vivacious and smart. She was on the cheerleading squad, graduated in the top of her class, and got a degree from Wake Forest. She eventually returned to Hallsboro, where she got married (I sang at her wedding), became the school librarian, and raised a family.

Van was the counterpart to Peggy. The house he grew up in was just around the corner from mine and across a little patch of woods behind Peggy's. He was a good athlete in high school and a scholar. After a stint in the military, he graduated from Wingate College and North Carolina State University, taught school, and coached for a while before going to work at Hercules, a chemicals manufacturer. In addition to Peggy, he, too, got married and raised a family.

All of us spent Sunday mornings and evenings, Wednesday nights, and spring and fall revivals at the Baptist church. It wasn't always fun, but we were always there.

⌒

I had asked Van and Peggy to join me for lunch that day to help me remember what had made our little town so special. (We all modestly agreed that the fact we grew up there made the town remarkable.)

In the course of the conversation, there were a lot of "do you remembers" and "whatever happened tos," but the gist of it all was that Hallsboro had been different from most other places we were familiar with in the South of our time—the 1950s and 60s. At least it was different from the places we'd read about in the newspapers and saw on television.

That day at the café, Peggy was still pretty, still vivacious, and still the epitome of "the girl next door" ... which she literally had been. As we all reminisced, she said, "Hallsboro was a safe place for me growing up. I guess it was because everything was familiar. We all knew each other, not just the names but the families and what they did. What they "did" meant not just their occupations but where they went to church and how often, who their relatives were, and whether or not they were 'good people.'"

"It was a time when you helped each other," added Van. "If a man needed help getting his crop in, we all pitched in to get it done. He didn't even have to ask."

It was a time some people would call *boring*. Nothing much happened that didn't happen every day. Our lives consisted of school, church, and work. That's not to say we didn't occasionally have some form of excitement.

One time my family's business, Council and Company, decided to have a big sales promotion at the store. Anybody who made a purchase of as much as five dollars on a particular Saturday would get a chance to win a goat, which was tied in an area beside the store. You had to be present to win, and so many of our customers gathered there and spent the day. At that time, all the stores in town stayed open until nine o'clock on Saturday night. By nine o'clock, a crowd of more than a hundred people were there for the drawing.

It didn't take much to draw a crowd in Hallsboro.

There were bigger events like the little circus that came to town and set up right behind the Pierce and Company store, beside Peggy's house. "It was so close I could hear the gorilla gumbling and rambling in his cage like he was right outside my window," Peggy laughed as we reminisced at Gwen's.

Then there was the time the traveling tent evangelist came to town and set up down in a field at the fork of the road that lead to Red Bug. Our mamas wouldn't let us go down there. We were Baptists; and Baptists, Methodists, and Presbyterians didn't attend such "rowdy" services. We didn't even attend each other's services!

On reflection, we had to acknowledge that even in the close-knit community there was a sub-strata, such subtle distinctions of society that we never thought about them, never consciously acknowledged them. Nobody had much money, so that was not a distinction. The churches were Christian, but each denomination was certain that their doctrinal beliefs were correct and would remain unchallenged by not hearing anything different.

I had talked to Billy Shipman just a few days before Van, Peggy, and I met for lunch. Billy lived, and had always lived, in a little section of the Hallsboro community called the Elbow. The name came about because the county road made a kinda half-circle (an elbow turn) off state road 1001, just south of town. It was a farming community but still very much a part of Hallsboro.

Billy was raised by an aunt and uncle. He too was a good student in high school. After graduation, he worked for Council and Company while saving his money for college. After graduating from the University of North Carolina at Wilmington, he got his master's degree and taught history at his Hallsboro alma mater. He later became principal of the school. He had also gone to the Baptist church.

"Sometimes on Saturday afternoon, some of us boys from the Elbow would go into Hallsboro just to be going," he said. "Sometimes we'd get in 'dirt-clod fights' with the Hallsboro boys, then get up a ball game somewhere. There was a distinction, but it was a friendly distinction."

That acknowledgement brought to mind a conversation I'd had just a few days earlier with another friend of mine. Carl Burney grew up in the Red Bug community. More specifically, his house was part of the black mill quarters, the collection of houses owned by the lumber companies that had been a vital part of the history of the area. We had not actually seen each other in several years until the day we met at the service station in Whiteville.

Carl had graduated from Artesia, the black school in Hallsboro. He completed his military duties and later served in law enforcement for several years before working with the paper company.

As usual, once old friends meet they start to reminisce about "the old days." Like Van, Peggy, Billy, and me, Carl said, "Hallsboro was a unique place back in the fifties and sixties when all the lumber mills were going strong. We weren't exactly isolated exactly, but we didn't have a lot of contact with folks outside our community. We didn't need anything else. There were five operational lumber mills, five general stores, two automobile repair shops, a dry cleaners, movie theater, service station, barber shops, an ice cream parlor, a fish market, plus two school houses and a bunch of churches. Just about anything you needed or wanted was right there in Hallsboro. The only thing we didn't have was a bank, but we really didn't need one since nobody had much money."

"And we all got along," he added.

And there was the distinction. We *all* got along, black and white. At a time when the news was filled with stories of marches and church bombings, we not only got along but worked together. That's not to say there were no inequities. At the movie theater, black folks were supposed to sit in the balcony. Sometimes, some of us white children would join our black friends there to watch the Saturday afternoon serials but it was never the other way around. We never thought about changing it. Both schools were grades one through twelve. The students at Artesia school got second-hand books, but they had excellent teachers, and many of their students went on to college; many even got advanced degrees, just like the white students.

Still, Hallsboro was not an Eden. In the midst of change in the 1960s, a boy named Gene Cheek was sent to Boys Home. The impetus was the fact that his mother had "took up" with a black man back in Winston-Salem. Even in the social service offices of the state, social justice was still over-shadowed by prejudice. And although Gene eventually accepted that the campus at Lake Waccamaw was the right place for him at the time, he did not go gently into that good night. He even fell in love and told the girl about his mother back in Winston-Salem. She told her family, and, as a result, the girl told Gene she couldn't see him anymore. Gene later wrote a book called *The Color of Love,* a catharsis for himself and a lesson for us. Hallsboro was not immune to prejudice, though we didn't exactly embrace it either. There is always some dust, even in the cleanest house.

The men who worked in the mills where Carl grew up were all paid the same low wages. The field hands on the farm were paid the same thing. And when the community decided they needed a fire station, they all got together and held community dinners, where black and white cooks roasted pigs and chickens, brought casseroles and piles of potato salad, pies and cakes, and gallons of sweet tea. And when the building was built and the new-used fire truck arrived, everybody celebrated with singing and more food at the new facility. Each of the church choirs presented special music. The Boone Sisters and the Hallsboro Men's Chorus sang their beautiful arrangements of gospel songs and my sister and I sang folk songs. And everybody ate and sang … together. The first fire chief was my father, and the assistant chief was Carl Bryant, a different Carl, though also a black man, who operated a used car and auto repair shop.

"We all knew we were different," my friend Carl Burney said, referring to the town's black community. "But we were more alike than different, and we all wanted the same thing: to take care of our families. Generally speaking, I guess we made the best of a bad situation, even if we didn't know it at the time."

I know that Carl, Peggy, Van, Billy, and I probably looked back on our youth in Hallsboro from a jaundiced perspective, probably more nostalgic than realistic. Nostalgia is heavily edited memory. But that's the way I want to remember it.

> *The sigh of the South wind stills the light,*
> *holding back the pressing night,*
> *as music floats on lilting wings,*
> *and the nesting red bird sings.*
>
> *Faces fade and memories slip,*
> *like misty shrouds 'round sailing ships,*
> *places veiled like a mourning shawl*
> *hiding times we can't recall.*
>
> *We shared the light the sun would send,*
> *we thought such light would never end.*
> *Time prevailed and dreams took flight,*
> *but, oh, it was a lovely light!*